D0871832

RAWN

TWENTIETH CENTURY INTERPRETATIONS OF

MOLLOY

MALONE DIES

THE

UNNAMABLE

A Collection of Critical Essays

Edited by

J. D. O'HARA

Prentice-Hall, Inc. *Englewood Cliffs, N. J.*

A SPECTRUM BOOK

Copyright © 1970 by Prentice-Hall, Inc., Englewood Cliffs, New Jersey. A SPEC-TRUM BOOK. All rights reserved. No part of this book may be reproduced in any form or by any means without permission in writing from the publisher. C–13-599555-8; P–13-599548-5. *Library of Congress Catalog Card Number 77-126824.* Printed in the United States of America.

Current printing (last number):
10 9 8 7 6 5 4 3 2 1

PRENTICE-HALL INTERNATIONAL, INC. (*London*)
PRENTICE-HALL OF AUSTRALIA, PTY. LTD. (*Sydney*)
PRENTICE-HALL OF CANADA, LTD. (*Toronto*)
PRENTICE-HALL OF INDIA PRIVATE LIMITED (*New Delhi*)
PRENTICE-HALL OF JAPAN, INC. (*Tokyo*)

Contents

TWENTIETH CENTURY
INTERPRETATIONS
OF

MOLLOY
MALONE DIES
THE UNNAMABLE

Introduction

by J. D. O'Hara

I'd be quite incapable of writing a critical introduction to my
own works.

—Samuel Beckett

Even more than most, our century is characterized by social, economic, political, racial, civil, national, and international warfare, by
the slow-motion collapse of social, political, and religious institutions,
and by the decay of personal and communal morality. Things have
fared no better within. To an optimistic earlier age Wordsworth pro-
claimed

> How exquisitely the individual Mind
> (And the progressive powers perhaps no less
> Of the whole species) to the external World
> Is fitted:—and how exquisitely, too—
> Theme this but little heard of among men—
> The external World is fitted to the Mind.

But in our century the psychologists have stripped the mind of nobility, of natural goodness, and even of competence in dealing with the
outside world. Scientists have found more and more discrepancies between what our senses report and what we thought they were perceiving. Philosophers have reduced wisdom to words and words to arbitrary
conventions. The external world has become alien to us. Most works
of literature reflect their age, and it is not surprising that in this abom-
inable century literature is didactic and escapist. It offers us, separately
or simultaneously, lectures on the state of our worlds and flights from
them into religion, pornography, nostalgia, or utopia.

Literature's highest function, however, has always been to clarify
existence by eliminating its trivia and arranging the highlights evoca-
tively, enabling us readers to undergo essential experiences rather than

the everyday varieties. James Joyce is dominant among those modern writers whose works make us experience existence rather than theorize about it, analyze it, label it, understand it, and avoid it. As Beckett wrote about *Finnegans Wake* in "Dante. . . Bruno. Vico. . Joyce," "His writing is not *about* something: *it is that something itself.*" [1]

In the essays that follow, Beckett will be linked with many writers. As a stylist, he is often compared with playwrights like Artaud, Ionesco, and Pirandello. He is credited with being a father of the anti-novel, especially as that genre has been developed in France. In his nonstop, bleakly witty colloquial monologues he reminds one of Joyce and Céline; Joycean again is his technical variety, his continuous experimentation with style. As an Irishman writing in France (and in French) he joins such exiles as Conrad, Nabokov, Joyce, and Pound. The philosophical content of his work connects him with the novel of ideas, especially as written by Sartre and Camus, with whom he is often grouped as another existentialist; the religious content leads to his being linked with Kirkegaard, Dostoyevsky, and Kafka. In short, many writers resemble Beckett in this or that respect; yet he resists pigeonholing. Like any first-rate writer, he is *sui generis* and exhausts his category.

Beckett insists on the perpetual presence of existence and subjects us to that presence. There is no naïveté about this: the *now* of this existence may have the physical world as its content, but equally it may consist of ideas, memories, or pure fiction. This existence is basically irrational, arbitrary, and beyond control. We perceive it along with narrators who are educated, intelligent, perceptive, articulate, crippled, and helpless. The experience of reading such a novel differs almost totally from that of reading the didactic and escapist novels that form the bulk ("put bulk in your diet") of our modern literature. Reading Beckett, we may experience parodies of didactic reasoning, but we learn nothing of practical use, and although we are immersed completely in the novel's report of existence, it is no escape from our own because it reminds us too often of our own. And we are taken utterly beyond race, nationality, politics, religion, society, morality, philosophy, and all such categories of experience. Some of these topics enter the novels, to be sure, but when they are illuminated by the attention of one of Beckett's speaking intelligences we see them for what they are, pitiful or ridiculous evi-

---

[1] Information about this and other works cited in the Introduction will be found in the Chronology (for Beckett) and the Selected Bibliography. All references to the trilogy will be to the Grove Press paperback edition (1965) and will be given in the text in all the essays here.

dence of man's perpetual attempts to find order and purpose in chaos. Accepting them as truth (which is what Moran does, at first) may permit one to evade existence for a while, but Moran's experience suggests that evasion is no escape.

Evasion is no escape: one of the persistent themes of Beckett's fiction from its earliest days. His characters pass the time, kill time, distract themselves from time with theological or mathematical speculations . . . but at their back they always hear time's wingless chariot on its treadmill, getting them nowhere toward death. A lifetime becomes a perpetually incomplete process, diversified at first by learning, travel, sex, and the desire for love, but dwindling at length into the mere existence of a mind sick with thought and fastened to a dying animal.

In short, Beckett's subject matter is painful and his insistence upon it unremitting, and he makes enormous demands upon his reader's attention and intelligence. Yet he is the foremost living writer of drama and fiction, and is acknowledged to be so not by any mere clique but by the general assent of the literary world.

This is an eminence he had no desire for and takes no interest in; after avoiding it for most of his life, he has had greatness thrust upon him unsought. For the first forty years of his life he passed as simply another member of that small but persistent class of people who are both eccentric and academic. During his early years the academic side dominated. He attended Portora Royal School, as had Oscar Wilde, and Trinity College, Dublin. There he won a scholarship and a gold medal and presented a research essay on the Convergistes. He received his M.A. in 1931, by which time he had already embarked upon his academic career, teaching at Campbell College, Belfast, at the Ecole Normale Supérieure in Paris, and at his alma mater. Meanwhile he published his fine monograph on Proust and his odd essay on Joyce. The M.A. was awarded him in December, 1931; in the same month he resigned from Trinity and ended his academic career. The eccentric side of his nature had not been dormant—there is no such group as the Convergistes, for instance, and a durable rumor has it that his resignation was written on toilet paper—but from this point on, it became dominant. Two years earlier he had published an odd short story in Eugene Jolas's *transition,* and a year later he won a prize with his odd poem about Descartes, *Whoroscope.* He also became a member of the Joyce circle. So when he dropped out of academia and returned to Europe, aged twenty-five, he already possessed all the credentials entitling him to the rank of minor literary eccentric, a career he pursued throughout the thirties. He kept up the association with Joyce, traveled through Europe, underwent an affair with Peggy Guggenheim, wrote the unfinished novel *Dream of Fair to Middling Women* and turned it into a collection of short stories, *More Pricks Than Kicks,* published an unnoticed novel, *Murphy,* wrote critical articles and minor poems, translated, drank, brooded, and in short lived as dozens of others were living, oddly and insignificantly, throughout Europe.

The war seems to have been behind Beckett's change from minor to major writer. He decided to wait it out in Paris rather than return to Ireland, and at first he apparently saw little to choose between Axis fascism and Allied corruption. When the Germans occupied Paris and began imprisoning and executing his friends, however, Beckett's neutrality ended and he joined a Resistance group. "Boy-scout stuff," he now calls that work, but it was dangerous, and he was soon forced to flee into unoccupied France, where from 1942 until the end of the war he posed as a farm laborer in the Vaucluse. *Watt,* the novel he wrote during that period ("to get away from war and occupation"), suggests that the change had begun. Superficially *Watt* resembles *Murphy* in recounting the adventures of a comic, pseudophilosophic seeker after certainties, with a background of more conventional comic figures inhabiting a fairly realistic world. The tone is harsher, however, as one might expect of a wartime novel; the events are often painfully grotesque; there is no outlet for sympathetic feeling similar to those provided in *Murphy* by Celia and the boy flying the tandem kites; and where Murphy was sought by the other characters, Watt is insulted, stoned, and disliked by most of them. Murphy insisted on the happiness of insanity; Watt, who ends in a sanitarium, is not noticeably happy. Finally, the tone of sardonic detachment that characterized *More Pricks Than Kicks* and *Murphy* is beginning to alter. It is difficult to say just how; Watt is kept at a distance from us, certainly, but the narrative itself seems to be troubled and to lack the glib assurance of *Murphy*'s. The narrator, who is named Sam and is also in the sanitarium, is detached from most of the events of the novel, but not from the world they typify.

What the war may have begun, Beckett's continued involvement with French life fostered. Although he had written some things in French earlier, he had regarded himself as an Irish writer until he finished *Watt*. After that novel, he began intensively to make himself into a French writer. Most of his early attempts dissatisfied him (though not for linguistic reasons). A play, *Eleutheria,* a novel, *Mercier et Camier,* and a *nouvelle,* "Premier Amour," remain unpublished; three other *nouvelles* were published and have since been translated (as "The Expelled," "The Calmative," and "The End").

The causes of Beckett's shift to French cannot be specified. Scholars have made some astute suggestions (see especially Coe, p. 14, and Fletcher, *Novels*, pp. 98f.), and Beckett's friend and publisher John Calder speaks with considerable authority when he says that "Beckett started to write in French in order to escape the richness of the Irish rhetoric. The discipline of writing in a much colder and exacting language is part of his general economy." But the final word rests with Beckett and is reported in the Notes on Contributors, *Transition forty eight* (1948): "Invited to give some account of his reasons for now writing in French, . . . he replied that he would be happy to do so and seemed then to have some views on the subject. But some months later he wrote saying that he did not know why he wrote in French, nor indeed why he wrote at all."

Other characteristics of those *nouvelles* are more interesting, especially if considered as preparation for the trilogy. They have remarkably little in common with Beckett's earlier fiction, for instance, although as John Fletcher has pointed out their common hero resembles Watt: "Like Watt, he is a milk-drinker, does not share the common phobia of rats, wears a heavy greatcoat. . . ." He is perhaps Watt with the more grotesque comic traits removed; he is certainly the second of that line of overcoated outcasts who will figure so prominently in the trilogy and *Waiting for Godot*. Murphy was sought by his fellows and Watt was scorned by them; the unnamed hero of the *nouvelles* exists on another level than the social. He is certainly an outcast—quite literally, in "The Expelled"—but when Fletcher points out that "we attain to a sharper realization of what it really means to be an outcast and a reject from society, and . . . how hypocritical and cruel our society appears to those who see it only from the gutter and dungheap" (*Novels*, p. 105), his remarks seem both true and irrelevant. The *nouvelles* foreshadow the trilogy in achieving a point of view from which mere social criticism is excluded. To blame the hero's plight on society (Fletcher does not) would be as absurd as blaming it on his nationality. It is existence itself that victimizes him.

Another characteristic of the *nouvelles* that helps us to understand why Beckett has described them as blueprints for the trilogy is the curious relationship among them, a relationship more easily sensed than specified. Fletcher tells us that "Beckett has said that they can be taken as three phases of one existence . . . : prime, death and limbo" (*Nov-*

els, p. 102), but they do not suggest their interrelationship in the conventional, straightforward manner of the *Forsyte Saga,* for instance. No place or personal names connect the stories, nor does the character allude to his existence in a previous story; our identification depends on small and not always consistent details of dress, body, and ideas. But our surest incentive to make this identification of character comes from our sense of his situation. The details change, but the tone of detached hopelessness remains; we encounter a discontinuous hero in a continuous plight, perhaps.

The most significant characteristic of the *nouvelles* (the implication that they are put together out of separable parts is merely academic, of course), most significant with regard to the trilogy especially, is the switch from third-person to first-person narration. The change has more implications than can be developed here, and indeed Beckett did not develop all of them in the *nouvelles.*

Of *More Pricks Than Kicks* Edwin Muir wrote that "the whole book is somewhat like extremely good and calculated and quite impossible talk." Like *At Swim-Two-Birds* and similar exploitations of erudition and Irish colloquial style mixed together, Beckett's early writing made comic profit out of the varied disparities of colloquial speech and erudite content, erudite speech and colloquial content, erudition in a colloquial context (as when Belacqua Shuah botches his toast-making: "He had burnt his offering, he had not fully dressed it. Yes, he had put the horse behind the tumbrel"), . . . and all these complications reported by an intrusive and self-conscious narrator ("This may be premature. We have set it down too soon, perhaps. Still, let it bloody well stand"). But the narrator manages this style and pose much better than the characters do and often at their expense, and so he interferes between them and us, as Fielding does in *Tom Jones.*

The first-person narration developed in the *nouvelles* preserves the characteristics of this self-conscious narrator and provides these continual reminders of the narrative's artificiality. "I must indeed have been moving fast, for I overhauled more than one pedestrian, there are the first men, without extending myself, I who in the normal way was left standing by cripples," says the hero of "The Calmative," pausing in midcareer to notice that adults have entered his tale for the first time. But since the narrator is now also the hero, the narrative now testifies by its voice as well as its content to the hero's life and mind. We are not separated from him by the style, though we are still detached from the immediate reality of his adventures by it. Or, more accurately, it is the narrating of the tale that constitutes its immediate reality, rather than the previously experienced adventures that the tale reports. (Stories told by Conrad's character Marlow often use this form.)

In a much-noted passage in *Tom Jones,* the narrator solemnly assures us that he has been unable to discover what, at one point, Tom ate for dinner. The remark's humor is based on our assumption that narrators are omniscient, at least in the sense that authors invent their stories and therefore can never be at a loss to know what happens in them. Of course novelists have frequently taken on themselves the task of communicating ideas through ignorant narrators, as in *Huckleberry Finn, Ulysses,* and "The Secret Sharer." Their method has been to put the character's perceptions in a context—of the work or life— that will contradict, modify, or supplement his limited point of view. Huck Finn approves of slavery, but we don't; Twain relies on our morality to correct Huck's. In *Ulysses,* Bloom at a Catholic mass watches communion: "The priest went along by them, murmuring, holding the thing in his hands. He stopped at each, took out a communion, shook a drop or two (are they in water?) off it and put it neatly into her mouth"—and Joyce relies on our knowledge of the mass to correct Bloom's misinterpretation of the priest's gesture. Again, Bloom contemplating his bowler thinks of "these pots we have to wear," and we are expected to recall, though he doesn't, the pots in the advertisement "What is home without Plumtree's Potted Meat? Incomplete. With it an abode of bliss."

Beckett too uses this device of the ignorant narrator, of course, as when Molloy fails to recognize the object he has stolen from Lousse as a kniferest, and when he asks, in passing, "Can it be we are not free? It might be worth looking into." But for the most part we may say that Beckett has removed the omniscient narrator and replaced him with an ignorant but uncorrectable narrating hero. In "The End," for instance, the hero tells us this:

> When I deemed that to tip my hat would suffice, I naturally did no more than tip it. But to tip one's hat is no easy matter either. I subsequently solved this problem, always fundamental in time of adversity, by wearing a kepi and saluting in military fashion, no, that must be wrong, I don't know, I had my hat at the end.

Here, what the hero does not know we do not know; we can never discover how he solved his hat-tipping problem. Furthermore, the Beckett narrator is not permitted to rewrite or omit what he does not understand; he is forced onward by the pressure of his narrative and can only insert a *perhaps, maybe, it seems,* or *I don't know,* leaving us to use these phrases ourselves.

This limitation of the ignorant narrator significantly affects our sense of his tale. An omniscient narrator, describing things unseen or unknown by the hero, necessarily creates a world external to and independent of that hero. But the world of a first-person narrative, like our own individual worlds, is necessarily solipsistic; nothing exists in it until perceived. Previously Beckett's seedy solipsists had wandered in a world that clearly existed without them and thereby disproved them. Now the thinking and perceiving mind, faulty though it is, is all in all. Its world is therefore like itself, faulty and incomplete, but Beckett makes no effort to improve and complete it. If we cannot do so ourselves, if the narrator's limitations are our own, then we are forced not merely to notice his ignorance as we notice Huck's or Bloom's, but to admit our own ignorance as well.

This ignorance, when it attempts to deal with fundamental issues, is Beckett's subject in the trilogy, *Molloy, Malone Dies, The Unnamable,* even more than in the *nouvelles.* He has expressed himself about it primarily in an interview he gave Israel Shenker:

> The kind of work I do is one in which I'm not master of my material. The more Joyce knew the more he could. I'm working with impotence, ignorance. I don't think ignorance has been exploited in the past. There seems to be a kind of esthetic axiom that expression is achievement— must be an achievement. My little exploration is that whole zone of being that has always been set aside by artists as something unuseable—as something by definition incompatible with art.
>
> I think that anyone nowadays, who pays the slightest attention to his own experience finds it the experience of a non-knower, a non-can-er. The other type of artist—the Apollonian—is absolutely foreign to me.

We have learned to read the fourth book of *Gulliver's Travels* as a satire on the mad critic who denies his own humanity while attacking the human race. It is equal madness for an author seriously to separate himself from his subject matter. Beckett had almost done this in *Murphy,* especially in such remarks as "All the puppets in this book whinge sooner or later, except Murphy, who is not a puppet." In *Watt* he had played with the pose of the ignorant narrator—"Watt

had a poor healing skin, and perhaps his blood was deficient in ? ."
—but the general effect remained that of an omniscient narrator
reporting from a distance on ignorant characters. The shift to first-
person narration eliminated this distance between narrator and character, and eliminated the omniscience as well.

The result is a narrating intelligence ignorant about life and art
and inhabiting a world limited by his ignorance of it. But from our
viewpoint this ignorance is so knowledgeable and is reported so skill-
fully by Beckett that we are almost never able to see beyond it. At
our best, we identify with the narrator; at worst, we learn from him
. . . and learn at the same time that our new knowledge is of no
use. "No denying it," the Unnamable says, "I'm confoundedly well
informed"; but he adds a few moments later, "No good wriggling,
I'm a mine of useless knowledge." And useless it is, or at least its
only use is to make clearer the opacity of life. Nevertheless, the
knowledge and intelligence in Beckett's works have led many readers
to treat them as cryptic wisdom literature, masking a gnomic Message.
Such a misunderstanding gave rise to one of the many *Godot*-like
canters scattered through interviews with Beckett; this is one con-
ducted by Gabriel d'Aubarède:

—Have contemporary philosophers exercised any influence on your
thought?
—I never read philosophers.
—Why not?
—I understand nothing of what they write.
—Nevertheless, one sometimes wonders if the preoccupation with the
problem of Being posed by the existentialists might not be a key to your
works . . .
—There is no key, there is no problem. If the subject of my novels could
be expressed in philosophic terms, I'd have had no reason to write them.
—And what *was* your reason for writing them?
—I don't know anything about it. I am not an intellectual. I am only a
sensibility. I conceived of Molloy and the rest the day I became aware of
my stupidity. Then I set out to write the things that I sensed.

When, in 1946, Beckett became aware of his ignorance and conceived the trilogy, the result was one of the most sustained and intense
creative outpourings in modern literature. Beckett told D'Aubarède
that he wrote them with extreme difficulty, "mais avec élan, dans une
sorte d'enthousiasme."

Basically the trilogy develops the point of view and habit of mind explored in the *nouvelles*, combined with that doubling of central character Beckett had practised in the abandoned *Mercier et Camier*. These central characters are cared for, bullied, rejected, isolated; they respond with ironic speculations and with feelings of rage, contempt, and curiosity; and they undergo manifold varieties of a few basic adventures. Fletcher compares the events of the French fiction to "a clown's act," adding that "the various episodes occurring in his history constitute the Beckettian clown's performance, each incident having become an unchanging item in his repertoire" (*Novels*, p. 128). The relation of his heroes to clowns is of long standing, of course; as early as "Yellow," in *More Pricks Than Kicks*, Beckett had listed "Bim and Bom, Grock, Democritus"—philosopher and clown together.

The funniest turns in the repertoire, if your taste runs to black humor, are those performed by the body. Molloy progresses, so to speak, from one-legged bicycling at the start to rolling and reptation at the end; Moran sets out on a bicycle at the start, and is about to set out on crutches at the end; Malone begins as a bed-ridden octogenarian and ends dead; the Unnamable, a weeping egg, conjures up surrogates who hobble on crutches or exist armless and legless in a jar. Moran tells us that he inclined his son's young mind "towards that most fruitful of dispositions, horror of the body and its functions"; comically expressed, that horror informs almost every bodily activity in the trilogy. Even the few lyrical moments connected with the body collapse into irony, as when Molloy celebrates the joy of crutches:

> There is rapture, or there should be, in the motion crutches give. It is a series of little flights, skimming the ground. You take off, you land, through the thronging sound in wind and limb, who have to fasten one foot to the ground before they dare lift up the other. And even their most joyous hastening is less aerial than my hobble. But these are reasonings, based on analysis. (64)

For Beckett as for Wordsworth, however, the mind is his haunt and the main region of his song. The mind, attached more or less flimsily to the body as the characters' hats are to their coats (Molloy speaks of "my soul's leap out to him, at the end of its elastic" [11]), is the place where life really happens in the trilogy. That mental life is too complex to be reduced to pattern here, of all places, but two topics at least deserve some comment: death and silence.

The repeated M and W of characters' names—Murphy, Watt,

Moran, Molloy, Malone, Macmann, Mahood, Worm—suggests some game on Beckett's part. Critics play one also, suggesting that M and W are tipped-over Σ, the Greek letter S, and that they all stand for Sam Beckett: this allows them to add Belacqua Shuah, Sam (*Watt's* narrator), Sapo, and Basil to their list. Well, maybe, we might say: Beckett's works are certainly not autobiographical, but we do sense a certain continuity behind them, and there is critical profit in this notion of a perpetual identity sequentially inhabiting diverse characters. It allows us to understand the death and rebirth of this perpetual identity as a metaphor.

Beckett used this metaphor as early as his monograph on Proust. One of his chief concerns there is to distinguish between two ways in which we experience life. One way is the drab existence of the creature thoroughly habituated to and numb to his environment. "Life is a succession of habits, since the individual is a succession of individuals. . . . Habit then is the generic term for the countless treaties concluded between the countless subjects that constitute the individual and their countless correlative objects." The second way of experiencing life occurs during "the periods of transition that separate consecutive adaptations, . . . when for a moment the boredom of living is replaced by the suffering of being."

Beckett's characters are subject to these continual changes, for which the most obvious metaphor is their bodily decay; and because of these changes they are continually or repeatedly obliged to feel the pain of being—which tempts them occasionally into grandiloquent remarks like Molloy's description of his life as "a veritable calvary, with no limit to its stations and no hope of crucifixion" (78). But there would seem to be major and minor changes, distinguishable by the extent of their effects upon the character. A major change, a major effort at readjustment, is signaled—this is all conjecture, of course—by a change of name and situation. Arsene's fine monologue in *Watt* speaks of a great alp of sand shifting almost imperceptibly but with impressive effect nevertheless; this is perhaps a metaphor for the minor changes. In *Proust* Beckett speaks of the major ones, and uses another metaphor: "the first and major mode is inseparable from suffering and anxiety— the suffering of the dying and the jealous anxiety of the ousted. The old ego dies hard." The death of the old ego, which Beckett also calls "the death of Habit," provides the image that allows us to understand a human life as a succession of lives experienced by the ego within the frame of a single physical life.

Beckett portrays this succession not "realistically," not psychologically, but metaphorically. His characters may recall violence done to them earlier; or their stories may begin with their waking suddenly to a consciousness of their new existence; and they sometimes end abruptly, unexpectedly. The death of the old ego is suggested in other ways, too, behind other situations. It helps to explain the fratricidal savagery with which Molloy kills the charcoal-burner, Moran kills his victim, and Malone's surrogate Lemuel attacks the picnickers. It suggests also why it should be that Molloy's victim resembles Molloy and Moran's, Moran. It expains why Moran should have been speaking, just before his victim improbably appeared, of his "growing resignation to being dispossessed of self" (149), and why he should remark, after killing the man, that "he no longer resembled me" (151). It is also worth noticing that both halves of *Molloy* end with the character's referring to himself in the detached third person. "Molloy could stay, where he happened to be," says Molloy; and Moran seems to distinguish between his present self and Moran: "I was getting to know [the voice] better now," he says; "It did not use the words that Moran had been taught when he was little . . ." In short, Beckett's characters sometimes suspect that they have died and are now in hell or purgatory, and they are; but they have also died and returned to life; or perhaps they have shed an old skin for a new one, like a snake—or an onion.

In the trilogy, then, death is frequently though not always, or not on all levels, a metaphor pointing to a mental event. Such events diversify existence for the characters, but their daily life consists of silence—a silence interrupted by, evaded by, shouted down by voices within the mind. Here again we are limited to metaphor. Molloy admits that what he has been calling a voice is really "something gone wrong with the silence"—something gone wrong with the equilibrium between the self and its habitual world: "somewhere something had changed, so that I too had to change, or the world too had to change, in order for nothing to be changed" (88). "The silence of which the universe is made," as Moran calls it (121), would seem to be the inhuman reality of stasis; and the imperative voices summon the self to that stasis. These voices are internal: Moran's Youdi and Obidil are too farcical for belief, and the Unnamable admits that the voices are simply an image (347).

Whatever these voices signify, it would seem better described as compulsion than desire; internal, they come in some sense from "outside," and they goad the character into doing things he has no desire to do. He naturally longs to shut them up, turn them off, and restore the silence. But there is another kind of voice too. This is the narrator's own (at least until the Unnamable begins to deny it), and it is his only protection against that silence—because silence, though it seems preferable to "them" and their nagging, is also terrifying. We are tempted to interpret this silence, and we should be: the image's apparent interpretability is an indication of its metaphoric value. But silence itself—listen!—is frightening enough; we may profitably leave the subject there until Mr. Fanizza takes it up again in his essay on *The Unnamable*.

Such, such are the joys of life in the trilogy. This life is not a philosopher's, despite D'Aubarède's conjecture. On the other hand, D'Aubarède is no fool; Beckett is steeped in philosophical notions and so are his writings.

No essay could take the census of philosophic ideas in his work, though many have dealt with this, that, or t'other one. A few notions will suffice as guides through the trilogy, however. One is Descartes' belief that there are three kinds of substance: God, spirit, and matter. The essence of spirit is thought; the essence of matter is extension in space. Since spirit and matter are essentially different, there is no connection between them except through God; since as God's creations we are essentially spirit, our bodies are irrelevant to us. Beckett's favorite Cartesian, Arnold Geulincx, wrote *ubi nihil vales, ibi nihil velis*: where you are worth nothing, there you should desire nothing; and spirit is worth nothing in the realm of matter. Also Cartesian is Beckett's means of discovering the self. *Cogito ergo sum*, thought Descartes: I think, therefore I am; thinking, I am aware of a *res cogitans*, a thing thinking, and that thing is the self. To these ideas should be added Bishop Berkeley's idealist assertion that matter has no existence except as a complex of experienced qualities in one's mind, that we exist only as similarly experienced by God, and that therefore *esse est percipi*: to be is to be perceived. (Beckett develops this idea especially in *Film*.) And finally we may include the assertion of phenomenologist Edmund Husserl that consciousness must always be consciousness *of* something.

Beckett puts these ideas together roughly as follows. Matter exists in space; spirit exists in time, in the flow of mental consciousness. Malone claims that he has been "nothing but a series or rather a succession of local phenomena all my life" (234). If a specific succession of local phenomena deserves to be named Molloy or Moran or Malone or Mahood, it is because something—the identity, the self—has remained constant despite or within this flux. Descartes told us that we intuit the existence of this *res cogitans* as well as its *cogitationes*. All well and good, until we add Berkeley and Husserl. Berkeley suggests that Being is created by external perception; Husserl claims that perception is always perception *of* something. If the self is perceived in the activity of thinking, then the self exists. But in perceiving the self we have externalized it, since perception is always perception of something: perception of our self is perception of a self outside us. What perceives that self? A deeper self, which, when itself perceived, becomes the object of yet another self's perception, and so on down to what Beckett calls "the ideal core of the onion." It's an old puzzle, old when Schopenhauer wrote that "the knower himself cannot be known precisely as such, otherwise he would be the known of another knower," but it has not lost its point or pain with age.

The alternative to this infinite regression seems to lie in agreeing with Malone that, as David Hume put it, mankind is "nothing but a bundle or collection of different perceptions, which succeed each other with an inconceivable rapidity, and are in a perpetual flux and movement" (*Treatise of Human Nature,* I, iv, i). Unfortunately Beckett's characters, including Malone, are kept from accepting this happy dissolution by the nature of thought, which forcibly conveys the existence of a perceiver as well as this flow of perceptions. At one point Molloy remarks, "I began to think, that is to say to listen harder" (61). This distinction between thought and the self, this duality of mental existence, has often been noticed. For instance, in *Adagia* Wallace Stevens says that "when the mind is like a hall in which thought is like a voice speaking, the voice is always that of someone else." And Prufrock's unspoken monologue begins, "Let us go then, you and I." We are left not merely with the existence of self as distinct from thought, but with the impossibility of expressing that self as thought.

The progress of the trilogy and indeed of Beckett's fiction is in large measure the peeling of the self toward its ideal core. To some extent the process is analogous to Husserl's phenomenological reduction. Just as he taught philosophers to "bracket" and set aside layers of experience, aiming at the structure of thought without its specific content, so the Beckett hero regresses from the social context of Murphy and even Watt, through Moran, Molloy, Malone, and Mahood to the soft egg of the Unnamable, peeling toward that possible impossible philosopher's man, the self at once expressed and potential, objective and subjective.

It is a search recognizably connected with some of the concerns of modern post-Cartesian idealism (cf. Heidegger's *Being and Time* and Sartre's *Being and Nothingness*). Heidegger is concerned to show the relationship between the Self and those elements Husserl stripped away. For this reason his chief topic is *Dasein* (Being-there). The term insists on a primary fact about the existence of any human: he comes to consciousness of himself as a Being already existing, already *there* in a world of objects and other humans to which and to whom he is related by time, by space, and by need. As is suggested by the phrase "consciousness of himself," he is also related to his *Dasein*. That is, his Self is divided. A man's Being-there in the world is not his total Being, his complete Self. For one thing he is continually tempted into inauthentic existence by Them: that is, by his notion of what other people as a group expect of him. Furthermore, he is largely in ignorance of what he potentially *is*. In the sense of Being as totality, he can never be complete until death, when he can no longer be conscious of himself; in the sense of Being as achieved Selfhood, he may never find his Self or, having found it, he may outlive his achievement without maintaining his Selfhood. Gloomy prospects everywhere, in short.

The chief threat to authentic Being is time. In Heidegger's philosophy the flow of future into past is a primary concern. His major villains are those who try to evade their search for Self—a search that would oblige them to face the guilt of unachieved Selfhood and the dread of death and of the nothingness into which all things go. They evade the search for Self by evading the future and living entirely in the flow of present moments—like T. S. Eliot's commuters, "distracted from distraction by distraction"—or else they accept the fixed inauthentic Self offered by Them and live in the public past, instead of projecting themselves toward their own personal, futural, inachievable Selfhood . . . and death.

Jean-Paul Sartre studied under Husserl when young, and like Heidegger he speaks of inauthenticity and dread. For the Beckett world, one of Sartre's chief topics derives from his study of Husserl. Sartre describes himself as a phenomenologist, but he takes sharp issue with a late development of Husserl's thought in which the older philosopher implied that the ego, the I, exists subjectively. In *The Transcendence of the Ego* Sartre opposes this notion and insists that the *I* is a creation of consciousness and is the object of that consciousness, whose perception the *I* transcends. Sartre's criticism takes us back not only to Husserl but to Descartes. Descartes' *cogito ergo sum* took thinking as evidence for the existence of a Self, an ego, the immaterial actor of the mental act. Not so, says Sartre. Cognition, as Husserl said, is always cognition *of* something. We cannot merely think; we must think of a chair, of tomorrow's lunch, or of that hateful fellow Paul. But these are impersonal thoughts at which no ego is present, says Sartre. The thought is not "I am conscious of a chair," but only "consciousness of a chair now *is*." Only when consciousness is turned on itself can it reflect on that previous consciousness and say "I was conscious of a chair." Pure consciousness sees hateful Paul; only reflective consciousness can say "I hate Paul." The *I*, then, is always the object, not the subject, of consciousness.

Sartre's conclusions seem the opposite of those suggested by Schopenhauer and Stevens, but the opposition is less significant, for our purposes, than the underlying agreement. One school of thought sees the Self as inescapably objective and unreachable, the other sees it as inescapably subjective and inexpressible; but both agree on an irreducible duality within our consciousness. Beckett's trilogy explores that duality.

But the existence of such concerns in the trilogy should not be misconstrued. If the subject of Beckett's novels could be expressed in philosophic terms, he'd have had no reason to write them. In the introduction to *A Vision*, his long and complex description of psychological and historical reality, Yeats tells his no doubt startled reader, "Some will ask whether I believe in the actual existence of my circuits of sun and moon." His answer is no. "If sometimes, overwhelmed by miracle . . . , I have taken such periods literally, my reason has soon recovered; and now that the system stands out clearly in my imagination I regard them as stylistic arrangements of experience comparable to the cubes in the drawing of Wyndham Lewis and to the ovoids in the sculpture of Brancusi." A significant number of modern writers, among them Conrad, Hardy, Wallace Stevens, and Joyce, have spent much of their time as Yeats did, creating systems of thought in which they do not believe, but which serve them as meaningful "stylistic arrangements of experience." Beckett seems to be among them. From his early *Whoroscope* through his latest plays, he has created a body of writings referring consistently to a philosophically described world.

In *Heart of Darkness* Conrad insisted on the necessity—if sanity and civilization are to be preserved—of "a deliberate belief." The phrase is paradoxical, since we generally assume that belief is involuntary. It expresses a recognition, ironically hedged in its context, of the necessity for what Camus sardonically called "the leap of faith," the acceptance of values and ideas that we know to be merely man-made and arbitrary. It is a leap that Beckett has always refused to take, however; philosophic ideas in his works are inevitably objects of irony, stylistic derangements of experience. Nevertheless, because his works so often allude to philosophic and theological ideas, that untaken leap exists importantly in his work as a perpetual temptation as well as an absurd impossibility. If the idea of God did not exist, no one could feel the painfulness of its absurdity; if the idea that life has meaning did not exist, the meaninglessness of life could hurt no one. But these ideas hurt Beckett, and to some extent he expresses that pain by fiction in which the godlessness and meaninglessness—innocuous in themselves—are made absurdly painful by perpetual reminders of nonexistent but conceivable alternatives. In Beckett's work these reminders are philosophic and theological, in part because such categories lie ready to his hand, but also because these disciplines promise the most to humanity. Few retellings of the story of Pandora explain why that box full of evil things should have contained hope among them. Some modern writers—see *The Nigger of the "Narcissus"*—understand that story, however, and Beckett is among them. It is because philosophy and theology foster hope that they make our lives so painful; it is their painfulness, not their truth, that makes them relevant to Beckett's concerns.

Where Beckett differs most from Yeats and the others, then, is in the intensity of his disbelief. The others, admitting that their arrangements of experience have only metaphoric validity, nevertheless imply that arrangement itself is a valid notion. Beckett makes no such implication. As he told Tom Driver, "When Heidegger and Sartre speak of a contrast between being and existence, they may be right, I don't know, but their language is too philosophical for me. I am not a philosopher. One can only speak of what is in front of him, and that now is simply the mess." The Unnamable, muttering about his old enemy "they," is less polite: "They must consider me sufficiently

stupefied with all their balls about being and existing," he says (348).
But he is not stupefied.

Ideas have forms, and these forms give their shape to all discursive
speech, even narratives. To take ideas ironically, as Beckett does, is
therefore to encounter as an artist formal problems unknown or
ignored in most art. For Beckett these problems have often seemed
almost obsessive. In his interview with Tom Driver he spoke at some
length, for him, about the tension between form, as a determining
characteristic of art, and "the mess," the chaos of art's subject matter
in our time. The tension exists for Beckett because he dislikes aesthetic
form that imposes order on chaos and thereby denies the existence
of that chaos. The form he approves, then (he doesn't claim to have
found it), "will be of such a type that it admits the chaos and does
not try to say that the chaos is really something else. The form and
the chaos remain separate. The latter is not reduced to the former.
That is why the form itself becomes a preoccupation, because it exists
as a problem separate from the material it accommodates. To find a
form that accommodates the mess, that is the task of the artist now."
   One approach toward such a form involves using an idea's formal
properties without regard to the credibility of the idea itself. Harold
Hobson reports Beckett's discussion of this approach:

> I am interested in the shape of ideas even if I do not believe in them.
> There is a wonderful sentence in Augustine. I wish I could remember the
> Latin. It is even finer in Latin than in English. "Do not despair; one of
> the thieves was saved. Do not presume; one of the thieves was damned."
> That sentence has a wonderful shape. It is the shape that matters.

A simple application of this approach provides the basis of Beckett's
Film. His script for that movie includes this preliminary assertion:

> *Esse est percipi.*
>   All extraneous perception suppressed, animal, human, divine, self-
> perception maintains in being.
>   Search of non-being in flight from extraneous perception breaking
> down in inescapability of self-perception.
>   No truth value attaches to above, regarded as of merely structural and
> dramatic convenience.

"It is the shape that matters," then, and not the truth of the shaping
idea. But for the reader, if not the writer, it is almost impossible to
experience an idea's shape detached from its content. Faith keeps

creeping in, unless shooed away by literary warnings. In the trilogy, these warnings may be reduced for our purposes to two types. The narrative shapes that Beckett employs—the detective-story pursuit in *Molloy,* for instance, and the writer-at-work in *Malone Dies*—are so conventional that the reader is never tempted to take them with complete seriousness. They give a form to the material they contain, but the reader repeatedly finds himself looking through that form rather than at it. (Similarly, the reader of Kafka's "Report to an Academy" or Orwell's *Animal Farm* sees through the talking-animal convention immediately, and is never tempted to read the story as if it were written by Thornton Burgess or Beatrix Potter.)

In *Molloy* most obviously, but in *Malone Dies* too, the form is also detached from its content by being treated ironically. The division of *Molloy*'s pursuit plot into two apparently independent parts, the failure of that pursuit, Malone's insistence on the insignificance of his stories, and their fragmentary quality, are all obvious signs of this ironic treatment. Equally, the unrealistic improbability or impossibility of the narrating itself in all three novels preserves the recognizable formal qualities of the first-person voice while discouraging us from any "realistic" credulity.

But increasingly within each section of *Molloy* and increasingly within each work as the trilogy goes on, as the formal elements are extended throughout the novel they tend to weaken and almost to disappear. Those initially realistic situations and concerns blur into nightmares of isolation, decay, panic, and violence; so that despite the formal elements we lose confidence in the possibility of predicting what will come. It is apparently this characteristic of his forms about which Beckett spoke to Shenker in distinguishing his own work from Kafka's: "You notice how Kafka's form is classic, it goes on like a steamroller—almost serene. It *seems* to be threatened the whole time —but the consternation is in the form. In my work there is consternation behind the form, not in the form. At the end of my work there's nothing but dust—the nameable."

In short, so far as the novels of the trilogy have recognizable forms, we can see Beckett simultaneously imposing and undercutting these forms. But he has developed other means of using ironically the formal characteristics of his writing. He has always insisted that he can be held responsible only for the barest skeleton of his works; speaking of *Endgame* he said, "If people want to have headaches among the overtones, let them. And provide their own aspirin." Nevertheless, he is careful to provide overtones as well as bones, and the overtones comprise some of the most interesting structural elements. Their most common function is allusiveness, of course. They widen and deepen the significance of a particular situation or character by encouraging us to relate it, more or less consciously, to similar situations or characters that we already take seriously. The example of *Ulysses* is relevant here; its extended Homeric parallel has no equivalent in Beckett's works, but the ironic nature of Joyce's serio-comic juxtaposition is also characteristic of Beckett's allusions.

What the *Odyssey* was for Joyce in *Ulysses*, the *Divine Comedy* is for Beckett in almost everything he writes. There are relatively few specific Dantean references in the trilogy, though Belacqua and Sordello make their almost ritual appearances; but the trilogy is pervaded with the atmosphere of the *Purgatory*, with hellish guards and policemen, and with the situation of Belacqua, obliged to relive his life on the antepurgatorial shore before he may begin ascending the mountain toward the Earthly Paradise. "It is only since I have ceased to live that I think of these things," says Molloy (25), who once had merely lived, "unsuspecting that one day, much later, I would have to go back over all these acts and omissions, dimmed and mellowed by age, and drag them into the eudemonistic slop" (55). Throughout the trilogy the characters wander, suffer, and tell their stories between the sea and St. John of God's, the ironic Earthly Paradise of this perpetual Purgatory where Beckett's characters struggle to discharge their eternal pensums.

The purgatorial situation has long interested Beckett; in "Dante . . . Bruno. Vico. Joyce" he described it with the exuberance of youth:

> In what sense, then, is Mr. Joyce's work purgatorial? In the absolute absence of the Absolute. Hell is the static lifelessness of unrelieved viciousness. Paradise the static lifelessness of unrelieved immaculation. Purgatory a flood of movement and vitality released by the conjunction of these two elements.

Absent even then from his conception of Purgatory was any sense of eventual release. To speak of living "on this earth that is Purgatory," Beckett asserted, is to say merely that "the machine proceeds. And no more than this: neither prize nor penalty; simply a series of stimulants to enable the kitten to catch its tail. And the partially purgatorial agent? The partially purged." This purgatorial restlessness, this desire to get on with it, causes the trilogy's characters to aim at stasis some of their most exasperated comments. "I was in peace for as long as I could endure peace," Molloy says (61); later he leaves the quiet of the seashore because "unfortunately there are other needs than that of rotting in peace" (76); and Moran asks, "Might not the beatific vision become a source of boredom, in the long run?" (167)

In themselves the details that comprise the trilogy's allusion to Dante are as insignificant as individual notes in music. It is their coherence as a motif that helps the reader to hear general significance in the particular stories of the trilogy—in this case, to hear the overtone of Dante's voice behind those of Beckett's characters. Needless to say, Beckett's allusions—here as elsewhere—are not always objectively faithful to their original contexts. The topics are sponsored by Dante; the opinions are not necessarily those of the sponsor.

Many other literary overtones are audible in the trilogy. Like Faust, the characters have studied and rejected all fields of knowledge (see for instance 39 and *sollst entbehren,* 110); and like Odysseus, they encounter many trials and temptations on their travels. But no source of allusions is so charming to Beckett as divine philosophy. Philosophy pervades the trilogy. Even Molloy's Faustian dismissal of all knowledge recalls Descartes' similar survey and dismissal at the start of his *Discourse on Method.* Some of these philosophic allusions are little more than grace notes: Geulincx's sailor, for instance (51, 336, 339, 392), or the hasty potshot at Camus: "But I do not think even Sisyphus is required to scratch himself, or to groan, or to rejoice, as the fashion is now, always at the same appointed places" (133). (Camus's *The Myth of Sisyphus* ends: "One must imagine Sisyphus happy.") Sometimes, however, the allusion is strong enough to give form to the situation in which it appears.

The beginning of *The Unnamable*—"Where now? Who now? When now?" etc.—owes something to the Narrator's comments about awakening, in the sixth paragraph of *Remembrance of Things Past;* but it also takes both form and meaning from a passage that concludes Hume's sceptical survey of knowledge in his *Treatise of Human Nature* (I, iv, vii):

Where am I, or what? From what causes do I derive my existence, and to what condition shall I return? Whose favour shall I court, and whose anger must I dread? What beings surround me? and on whom have I any influence, or who have any influence on me? I am confounded with all these questions, and begin to fancy myself in the most deplorable condition imaginable, inviron'd with the deepest darkness, and utterly depriv'd of the use of every member and faculty.[2]

Similarly, the character Worm gains meaning from our recollection of Lucian's "Philosophies for Sale" dialogue:

> *9th BUYER.* . . . What do you consider the end result of your philosophy [scepticism]?
> *PYRRHO.* Ignorance, deafness, blindness.
> *9th BUYER.* You mean the lack of both sight and hearing?
> *PYRRHO.* And of judgment and feeling. In short, being exactly like a worm.

These textual allusions and these sources seem to be fairly specific. Sometimes Beckett's allusiveness is more general in its source and more widespread in its textual location. Consider, for instance, the appearance of his characters. They are generally thought of as bums, at least since Roger Blin's premiere production of *Waiting for Godot*, but they may be seen more clearly in another light. They are sceptics, as I have already suggested, but they are cynics as well; and like the Greek cynics described by Lionel Casson they have the custom of "dressing in rags, living off scraps, and limiting their possessions to the old coat, sack, and staff which were the standard accoutrements of their order. . . . Since they made a point of disregarding personal appearance, they were singularly unappetizing to look at, and this may be responsible for their name (*kynikos* in Greek means 'doglike')." It is surely no accident that P. H. Solomon was able to write an article on dog images in *Molloy*.

As I have demonstrated, the notion of irony is frequently belabored by critics seeking to describe Beckett's works, even superficially, and

---

[2] The skeptical reader will recognize that this passage, like others cited, is merely a tentative suggestion of source. Beckett's allusiveness is complex and evocative; with practice, the reader can find or invent precursors everywhere. As a source for the opening of *The Unnamable* I have cited Proust and Hume, but consider this speech: "I was unformed in mind; I was dependent on none and related to none. 'The path of my departure was free,' and there was none to lament my annihilation. My person was hideous and my stature gigantic. What did this mean? Who was I? What was I? Whence did I come? What was my destination? These questions continually recurred, but I was unable to solve them." It is the monster speaking, in *Frankenstein*, Chapter 15. There is also the difficulty that Beckett conceives of allusiveness quite differently. In his introduction to an edition of *Godot*, Colin Duckworth says that "It would be pointless to maintain that Beckett places his characters in Dante's Purgatory. When I mentioned the possibility to Mr Beckett, his comment was characteristic: 'Quite alien to me, but you're welcome.'"

confronting over and over again the sense that things aren't what they seem to be. The overtones come and go all too transiently: we may strongly suspect that St. John of God's is an allusion to the Earthly Paradise—it has the same invariable breeze and improbable river, and it's called "a little Paradise" (277)—but we cannot generalize from this suspicion and say that *Malone Dies* is a modern *Purgatory*, any more than Molloy's encounter with Nausicaa (75) allows us to generalize *Molloy* into another *Odyssey* or *Ulysses*. In short, we cannot ignore the realistic level of the novels in favor of a shaping allegorical level, as we can in reading *Pilgrim's Progress*. On the other hand, that realistic level paradoxically discourages credulity. It's not simply that Malone couldn't have written the whole novel with one pencil stub or that Molloy wouldn't have bothered writing anything at all; the characters themselves are essentially incredible. Readers of *The Excursion* could never reconcile themselves to the notion that all those ideas came from a mere peddler, and such a circumstantially described peddler at that. Beckett's readers do not complain as publicly as Wordsworth's, but no one raised within the Protestant ethic will believe that such well-spoken, well-educated men as Molloy, Moran, and Malone could come down from everything to nothing. And even if they had so fallen, they would have quite different stories to tell, stories of psychological weakness, treacherous business associates, alcoholism, and so on. In short, characterization and situation share the ironic, unreliable nature of the overtones, leaving us no level of understanding on which we may perch with confidence.

A long aside seems obligatory here. In discussing characterization I have avoided mentioning the Unnamable, and for good reason. The Unnamable is . . . After thousands of words, Beckett could not finish that sentence, and yet an editor must make his pitiful attempt. The Unnamable is . . . perhaps . . . the nondimensional inner part of a Being, a Self, an individual fictional character whose external part is named Mahood. (The novel's title in manuscript was *Mahood*.) Mahood has objective existence; he is there; he can be named by the Unnamable. *Je est un autre,* said Rimbaud. Jorge Luis Borges has written a first-person fiction titled "Borges and I." In Sartrean terms Rimbaud's "je," Borges' "Borges," and the Unnamable's Mahood are all objects of self-consciousness. They have objective existence, while Mahood's consciousness (to pick a term at random) must by definition and function remain subjective, inexpressible, unnamable. This being so, or being postulated as so ("No truth value attaches to above, regarded as of merely structural and dramatic convenience"), the Unnamable can have no exterior and indeed can have no material existence at all. Whether he describes himself as a bearded egg or projects himself into a jar or into Worm, the physical result is as absurd as the attempt; Beckett is, among other things, giving comic expression to the idea that existence is a material matter.

We have heard Beckett contrasting Kafka's form, which is able to contain the "consternation," with his own, in which "there is consternation behind the form, not in the form." The sense of his comment seems to be that in his own works the consternation—perhaps to be understood with reference to the chaos of experienced reality—tends to undermine the formal qualities of his work. We have seen ways in which those formal qualities seem to be unstable and unreliable; since these novels are first-person narratives, it is tempting to think of imitative form and to say that the characters' psychological instability is mirrored in their narration. Grammar, however, forbids. There may be consternation behind the forms of Beckett's trilogy, but there is one place, at least, where the term seems inappropriate. The sentences in which his characters express themselves are beautiful. They may discuss consternation, they may even feel consternated, but Beckett's heroes never stoop to the creation of a poorly formed cry of despair. (Probably conclusive in showing that Malone dies at the end of his novel is the fact that his last sentence is grammatically imperfect.) On the other hand, we are not to assume that the characters' suffering is mitigated by the eloquence with which they express it. In *Rasselas* the prince utters a long, plaintive speech about his sorrows, "yet with a look that discovered him to feel some complacence in his own perspicacity, and to receive some solace of the miseries of life, from consciousness of the delicacy with which he felt, and the eloquence with which he bewailed them." Beckett was asked once if his characters could be said to feel a similar solace. His answer was flat and final: "No."

We have lingered so long over this hasty sketch of form in the trilogy because so many of Beckett's readers take a more conventional approach to his works, looking for their meaning or moral, as if they were Aesop's fables, or searching with D'Aubarède for the key that might unlock the trilogy and loose all its secrets. Beckett, who seems to know what he is doing, always insists that this approach is pointless; and he speaks often about form. To analyze form is to analyze how something is said rather than what is said. What the characters and situations of the trilogy "mean" at any one point, though puzzling questions, are not beyond all conjecture; how all these specific meanings take on tone and coherence from their formal existence within a work of art is a much more complex matter. Yet it seems probable that much future work on Beckett will be concerned primarily with the how, rather than the what. And why not? Few writers have complex messages for the world, and few messages are original, and fewer still are attended to. In the long run, what is being said is of minor interest, while how it is said may make it last for centuries. It is language we readers worship, not truth.

The Nightmare Life in Death

by Northrop Frye

In every age the theory of society and the theory of personality have closely approached each other. In Plato the wise man's mind is a dictatorship of reason over appetite, with the will acting as a thought police hunting down and exterminating all lawless impulses. The ideal state, with its philosopher-king, guards and artisans, has the corresponding social form. Michael explains to Adam in *Paradise Lost* that tyranny must exist in society as long as passion dominates reason in individuals, as they are called. In our day Marxism finds its psychological counterpart in the behaviorism and conditioned reflexes of Pavlov, and the Freudian picture of man is also the picture of western Europe and America, hoping that its blocks and tensions and hysterical explosions will settle into some kind of precarious working agreement. In this alignment religion has regularly formed a third, its gods and their enemies deriving their characteristics from whatever is highest and lowest in the personal-social picture. A good deal of the best fiction of our time has employed a kind of myth that might be read as a psychological, a social, or a religious allegory, except that it cannot be reduced to an allegory, but remains a myth, moving in all three areas of life at once, and thereby interconnecting them as well. The powerful appeal of Kafka for our age is largely due to the way in which such stories as *The Trial* or *The Castle* manage to suggest at once the atmosphere of an anxiety dream, the theology of the Book of Job, and the police terrorism and bureaucratic anonymity of the society that inspired Freud's term "censor." It was the same appeal in the myth of *Waiting for Godot* that, so to speak, identified Samuel Beckett as a contemporary writer.

As a fiction writer Samuel Beckett derives from Proust and Joyce,

"The Nightmare Life in Death" by Northrop Frye. From The Hudson Review *13* (*Autumn 1960*): *442–49. Copyright © 1960 by The Hudson Review, Inc. Reprinted by permission of The Hudson Review, Inc.*

and his essay on Proust is a good place to start from in examining his own work. This essay puts Proust in a context that is curiously Oriental in its view of personality. "Normal" people, we learn, are driven along through time on a current of habit-energy, an energy which, because habitual, is mostly automatic. This energy relates itself to the present by the will, to the past by voluntary or selective memory, to the future by desire and expectation. It is a subjective energy, although it has no consistent or permanent subject, for the ego that desires now can at best only possess later, by which time it is a different ego and wants something else. But an illusion of continuity is kept up by the speed, like a motion picture, and it generates a corresponding objective illusion, where things run along in the expected and habitual form of causality. Some people try to get off this time machine, either because they have more sensitivity or, perhaps, some kind of physical weakness that makes it not an exhilarating joyride but a nightmare of frustration and despair. Among these are artists like Proust, who look behind the surface of the ego, behind voluntary to involuntary memory, behind will and desire to conscious perception. As soon as the subjective motion-picture disappears, the objective one disappears too, and we have recurring contacts between a particular moment and a particular object, as in the epiphanies of the madeleine and the phrase in Vinteuil's music. Here the object, stripped of the habitual and expected response, appears in all the enchanted glow of uniqueness, and the relation of the moment to such an object is a relation of identity. Such a relation, achieved between two human beings, would be love, in contrast to the ego's pursuit of the object of desire, like Odette or Albertine, which tantalizes precisely because it is never loved. In the relation of identity consciousness has triumphed over time, and destroys the prison of habit with its double illusion stretching forever into past and future. At that moment we may enter what Proust and Beckett agree is the only possible type of paradise, that which has been lost. For the ego only two forms of failure are possible, the failure to possess, which may be tragic, and the failure to communicate, which is normally comic.

In the early story *Murphy*, the hero is an Irishman with an Irish interest in the occult—several of Beckett's characters are readers of AE —and a profound disinclination to work. We first meet him naked, strapped to a chair, and practising trance. He has however no interest in any genuine mental discipline, and feels an affinity with the easygoing Belacqua of Dante's *Purgatorio*, also mentioned in *Molloy*, who was in no hurry to begin his climb up the mountain. What he is really looking for is a self-contained egocentric consciousness, "windowless, like a monad," that no outward events can injure or distort. He is prodded by the heroine Celia into looking for a job, and eventually finds one as a male nurse in a lunatic asylum. In the asylum he discovers a kinship with the psychotic patients, who are trying to find the same thing in their own way, and his sympathy with them not only gives him a job he can do but makes him something rather better than a "seedy solipsist." To take this job he turns his back on Celia and other people who are said to need him, but in the airless microcosm of his mental retreat there is the one weak spot that makes him human and not completely selfish, a need for communication. He looks for this in the eye of Endon, his best friend among the patients, but sees no recognition in the eye, only his own image reflected in the pupil. "The last Mr. Murphy saw of Mr. Endon was Mr. Murphy unseen by Mr. Endon." He then commits suicide. The same image of the unrecognizing eye occurs in the one-act play *Embers* and in *Krapp's Last Tape,* where Krapp, more completely bound to memory and desire than Murphy, and so a figure of less dignity if also of less absurdity, looks into his mistress's eyes and says "Let me in." Another echo in this phrase will meet us in a moment.

The figure of the pure ego in a closed auto-erotic circle meets us many times in Beckett's masturbating, carrot-chewing, stone-sucking characters. A more traditional image of the consciousness goaded by desire or memory (an actual goad appears in one of Beckett's pantomimes), is that of master and servant. Already in *Murphy* we have, in the characters Neary and Cooper, an adumbration of the Hamm and Clov of *Endgame,* a servant who cannot sit and a master who cannot stand, bound together in some way and yet longing to be rid of each other. *Watt* tells the story of a servant who drifts into a house owned by a Mr. Knott, one of a long procession of servants absorbed and expelled from it by some unseen force. Technically the book is a contrast to *Murphy,* which is written in an epigrammatic wisecracking style. In *Watt* there is a shaggy-dog type of deliberately misleading humor, expressing itself in a maddeningly prolix pseudo-logic. One notes the use of a device more recently popularized by Lawrence Durrell, of putting some of the debris of the material collected into an appendix. "Only fatigue and disgust prevented its incorporation," the author demurely informs us. The most trivial actions of Watt, most of which are very similar to those we perform ourselves every day, are exhaustively catalogued in an elaborate pretence of obsessive realism, and we can see how such "realism" in fiction, pushed to so logical a conclusion, soon gives the effect of living in a kind of casual and unpunishing hell. Watt finally decides that "if one of these things was worth doing, all were worth doing, but that none was worth doing, no, not one, but that all were unadvisable, without exception."

In *Waiting for Godot*, as everyone knows, two dreary men in bowler hats stand around waiting for the mysterious Godot, who never appears but only sends a messenger to say he will not come. It is a favorite device of ironic fiction, from Kafka to Menotti's opera *The Consul*, to make the central character someone who not only fails to manifest himself but whose very existence is called in question. The two men wonder whether in some way they are "tied" to Godot, but decide that they probably are not, though they are afraid he might punish them if they desert their post. They also feel tied to one another, though each feels he would do better on his own. They resemble criminals in that they feel that they have no rights: "we got rid of them," one says, and is exhorted by a stage direction to say it distinctly. They stand in front of a dead tree, speculating, like many of Beckett's characters, about hanging themselves from it, and one of them feels an uneasy kinship with the thieves crucified with Christ. Instead of Godot, there appears a diabolical figure named Pozzo (pool: the overtones extend from Satan to Narcissus), driving an animal in human shape named Lucky, with a whip and a rope. Lucky, we are told, thinks he is entangled in a net: the image of being fished for by some omnipotent and malignant angler recurs in *The Unnamable*. In the second act the two turn up again, but this time Pozzo is blind and helpless, like Hamm in *Endgame*.

When the double illusion of a continuous ego and a continuous causality is abolished, what appears in its place? First of all, the ego is stripped of all individuality and is seen merely as representative of all of its kind. When asked for their names, one of the two men waiting for Godot answers "Adam," and the other one says: "At this place, at this moment of time, all mankind is us." Similar echoes are awakened by the Biblical title of the play *All that Fall*, with its discussion of the falling sparrow in the Gospels and its final image of the child falling from the train, its death unheeded by the only character who was on the train. Other characters have such names as Watt, Knott and Krapp, suggestive of infantile jokes and of what in *Molloy* are called "decaying circus clowns." The dramatic convention parodied in *Waiting for Godot* is clearly the act that killed vaudeville, the weary dialogue of two faceless figures who will say anything to put off leaving the stage. In the "gallery of moribunds" we are about to examine there is a series of speakers whose names begin with M, one of whom, Macmann, has the most obvious everyman associations. In this trilogy, however, there is a more thoroughgoing examination of the unreality of the ego, and one which seems to owe something to the sequence of three chapters in *Finnegans Wake* in which Shaun is studied under the names Shaun, Jaun and Yawn, until he disappears into the larger form of HCE. It is the "Yawn" chapter that Beckett most frequently refers to. In reading the trilogy we should keep in mind the remark in the essay on Proust that "the heart of the cauliflower or the ideal core of the onion would represent a more appropriate tribute to the labours of poetical excavation than the crown of bay."

Molloy is divided into two parts: the first is Molloy's own narrative; the second is the narrative of Jacques Moran, who receives a message through one Gaber from an undefined Youdi to go and find Molloy. The echoes of Gabriel and Yahweh make it obvious by analogy that the name "Godot" is intended to sound like "God." Youdi, or someone similar to him, is once referred to as "the Obidil," which is an anagram of libido. The associations of Molloy are Irish, pagan, and a Caliban-like intelligence rooted in a disillusioned sensitivity. Moran is French, nominally Christian, and a harsher and more aggressive type of sterility. Molloy, like many of Beckett's characters, is so crippled as to resemble the experiments on mutilated and beheaded animals that try to establish how much life is consistent with death. He is also under a wandering curse, like the Wandering Jew, and is trying to find his mother. There are echoes of the wandering figure in Chaucer's *Pardoner's Tale,* who keeps knocking on the ground with his staff and begging his mother to let him in. But Molloy does not exactly long for death, because for him the universe is also a vast auto-erotic ring, a serpent with its tail in its mouth, and it knows no real difference between life and death. Overtones of Ulysses appear in his sojourn with Lousse (Circe), and the mention of "moly" suggests an association with his name. He is also, more Biblically, "in an Egypt without bounds, without infant, without mother," and a dim memory of Faust appears in his account of various sciences studied and abandoned, of which magic alone remained. Like the contemporary beats (in *Murphy*, incidentally, the padded cells are called "pads"), he finds around him a world of confident and adjusted squares, who sometimes take the form of police and bully him. "They wake up, hale and hearty, their tongues hanging out for order, beauty and justice, baying for their due." The landscape around him, described in terms similar to Dante's Inferno, changes, but he is unable to go out of his "region," and realizes that he is not moving at all. The only real change is a progressive physical deterioration and a growing loss of such social contact as he has. The landscape finally changes to a forest and Molloy, too exhausted to walk and unable, like Beckett's other servants, to sit, crawls on his belly like a serpent until he finally stops. He arrives at his mother's house, but characteristically we learn this not from the last sentence but from the first one, as the narrative goes around in a Viconian circle.

Just before the end of his account, Molloy, who hears voices of "prompters" in his mind, is told that help is coming. Moran sets off to find Molloy, aware that his real quest is to find Molloy inside himself, as a kind of Hyde to his Jekyll. He starts out with his son, whom he is trying to nag into becoming a faithful replica of himself, and he ties his son to him with a rope, as Pozzo does Lucky. The son breaks away, Moran sees Molloy but does not realize who he is, and gets another order to go back home. He confesses: "I was not made for the great light that devours, a dim lamp was all I had been given, and patience without end, to shine it on the empty shadows." This ignominious quest for self-knowledge does not find Molloy as a separate entity, but it does turn Moran into a double of Molloy, in ironic contrast to his attitude to his son. Various details in the imagery, the bicycle that they both start with, the stiffening leg, and others, emphasize the growing identity. Moran's narrative, which starts out in clear prose, soon breaks down into the same associative paragraphless monologue that Molloy uses. The quest is a dismal failure as far as Moran and Molloy are concerned, but how far are they concerned? Moran can still say: "What I was doing I was doing neither for Molloy, who mattered nothing to me, nor for myself, of whom I despaired, but on behalf of a cause which, while having need of us to be accomplished, was in its essence anonymous, and would subsist, haunting the minds of men, when its miserable artisans should be no more."

The forest vanishes and we find ourselves in an asylum cell with a figure named Malone, who is waiting to die. Here there is a more definite expectation of the event of death, and an awareness of a specific quantity of time before it occurs. Malone decides to fill in the interval by telling himself stories, and the stories gradually converge on a figure named Macmann, to whom Malone seems related somewhat as Proust is to the "Marcel" of his book, or Joyce to Stephen and Shem.

Here an ego is projecting himself into a more typical figure (I suppose
Malone and Macmann have echoes of "man alone" and "son of man,"
respectively, as most of the echoes in Beckett's names appear to be
English), and Macmann gradually moves into the cell and takes over
the identity of Malone. Malone dreams of his own death, which is
simultaneously occurring, in a vision of a group of madmen going for
a picnic in a boat on the Saturday morning between Good Friday and
Easter, a ghastly parody of the beginning of the *Purgatorio*. Dante's
angelic pilot is replaced by a brutal attendant named Lemuel, a de-
stroying angel who murders most of the passengers.

In *The Unnamable* we come as near to the core of the onion as it is
possible to come, and discover of course that there is no core, no undi-
vidable unit of continuous personality. It is difficult to say just where
or what the Unnamable is, because, as in the brothel scene of *Ulysses*,
his fluctuating moods create their own surroundings. One hypothesis
is that he is sitting in a crouched posture with tears pouring out of his
eyes, like some of the damned in Dante, or like the Heraclitus who
became the weeping philosopher by contemplating the flowing of all
things. Another is that he is in a jar outside a Paris restaurant opposite
a horsemeat shop, suspended between life and death like the sibyl in
Petronius who presides over *The Waste Land*.

Ordinarily we are aware of a duality between mind and body, of
the necessity of keeping the body still to let the mind work. If we sit
quietly we become aware of bodily processes, notably the heartbeat
and pulse, carrying on automatically and involuntarily. Some religious
disciplines, such as yoga, go another stage, and try to keep the mind
still to set some higher principle free. When this happens, the mind
can be seen from the outside as a rushing current of thoughts and
associations and memories and worries and images suggested by desire,
pulsating automatically and with all the habit-energy of the ego behind it. Each monologue in the trilogy suggests a mind half-freed from
its own automatism. It is detached enough to feel imprisoned and
enslaved, and to have no confidence in any of its assertions, but immediately to deny or contradict or qualify or put forward another hypothesis to whatever it says. But it is particularly the monologue of
The Unnamable, an endless, querulous, compulsive, impersonal babble, much the same in effect whether read in French or in English,
and with no purpose except to keep going, that most clearly suggests a
"stream of consciousness" from which real consciousness is somehow
absent. *The Unnamable* could readily be called a tedious book, but

its use of tedium is exuberant, and in this respect it resembles *Watt.*

The Unnamable, who vaguely remembers having been Malone and Molloy, decides that he will be someone called Mahood, then that he will be something called Worm, then wonders whether all his meditations really are put into his mind by "them," that is, by Youdi and the rest, for his sense of compulsion easily externalizes itself. If he knows anything, it is that he is not necessarily himself, and that it was nonsense for Descartes to infer that he was himself because he was doubting it. All Beckett's speakers are like the parrot in *Malone Dies,* who could be taught to say "Nihil in intellectu," but refused to learn the rest of the sentence. All of them, again, especially Malone, are oppressed by the pervasive lying of the imagination, by the way in which one unconsciously falsifies the facts to make a fiction more symmetrical. But even Malone begins to realize that there is no escape from fiction. There are no facts to be accurately described, only hypotheses to be set up: no choice of words will express the truth, for one has only a choice of rhetorical masks. Malone says of his own continuum: "I slip into him, I suppose in the hope of learning something. But it is a stratum, strata, without debris or vestiges. But before I am done I shall find traces of what was."

In *The Unnamable,* as we make our way through "this sound that will never stop, monotonous beyond words and yet not altogether devoid of a certain variety," the Unnamable's own desire to escape, to the extent that he ever formulates it as such, communicates itself to us. The tired, tireless, hypnotic voice, muttering like a disembodied spirit at a seance, or like our own subconscious if we acquire the trick of listening to it, makes us feel that we would be ready to try anything to get away from it, even if we are also its prisoner. There is little use going to "them," to Youdi or Godot, because they are illusions of personality too. Conventional religion promises only resurrection, which both in *Murphy* and in the Proust essay is described as an impertinence. But "beyond them is that other who will not give me quittance until they have abandoned me as inutilizable and restored me to myself." That other must exist, if only because it is not here. And so, in the interminable last sentence, we reach the core of the onion, the resolve to find in art the secret of identity, the paradise that has been lost, the one genuine act of consciousness in the interlocking gyres (the Dante-Yeats image is explictly referred to) of automatism:

> . . . the attempt must be made, in the old stories incomprehensibly **mine,** **to** find his, it must be there somewhere, it must have been mine, before

being his, I'll recognize it, in the end I'll recognize it, the story of the
silence that he never left, that I should never have left, that I may never
find again, that I may find again, then it will be he, it will be I, it will be
the place, the silence, the end, the beginning, the beginning again . . .

Many curiously significant remarks are made about silence in the
trilogy. Molloy, for example, says: "about me all goes really silent,
from time to time, whereas for the righteous the tumult of the world
never stops." The Unnamable says: "This voice that speaks, knowing
that it lies, indifferent to what it says, too old perhaps and too abased
ever to succeed in saying the words that would be its last, knowing
itself useless and its uselessness in vain, not listening to itself but to
the silence that it breaks." Only when one is sufficiently detached from
this compulsive babble to realize that one is uttering it can one
achieve any genuine serenity, or the silence which is its habitat. "To
restore silence is the role of objects," says Molloy, but this is not Beckett's final paradox. His final paradox is the conception of the imaginative process which underlies and informs his remarkable achievement.
In a world given over to obsessive utterance, a world of television and
radio and shouting dictators and tape recorders and beeping space
ships, to restore silence is the role of serious writing.

Moran–Molloy: The Hero as Author

by Edith Kern

Molloy is not only the titular hero of Beckett's novel. Nor is he merely a literary convenience, an invention on the part of Beckett, to supply him with the appropriate "I" for his story. As most perceptive readers have noted, Molloy is an author consciously engaged in literary creation. To him writing is more than a pastime, more than a concern to record for posterity the memory of his strange journey. Writing is his only *raison d'etre*. For that purpose he was rescued from a ditch, into which he had fallen more dead than alive, by those mysterious forces that, in times of need, come to the aid of heroes. His trials served but to lead him to his "mother's room," where writing is identical with existence and existence means writing.

We first encounter Molloy after his arrival in this room. In its dim vacuity, into which scarcely a sound penetrates, Molloy vegetates, "formulates his thoughts," and without "much will left," wants to finish dying—though first he must write. The objects and human figures he conjures up are, like himself, detached from time and place. Seen out of all familiar context, they appear puzzling and purposeless. The men and women he introduces are now old, now young. Some are completely anonymous, referred to only as A or C. About the names of others Molloy is uncertain. As for himself, he has long been aware of a dense anonymity enfolding him, and barely remembers his name: ". . . even my sense of identity was wrapped in a namelessness often hard to penetrate. . . ." (31)

The symbolism of Molloy's arrival can be understood only in the light of the entire journey and in the perspective of his departure. Yet we are not told by Molloy when and from where he set out. One day, he merely recalls, "having waked between eleven o'clock and

"Moran–Molloy: The Hero as Author" by Edith Kern. *From* Perspective *11 (Autumn 1959): 183–93. Copyright © 1959 by Perspective, Inc. Reprinted by permission of Perspective, Inc.*

midday (I heard the angelus, recalling the incarnation shortly after) I resolved to go and see my mother." (15) He gives us vaguely to understand that there was an existence prior to the one he describes, when he used to be intelligent and quick (25); when he perhaps had a son to whom he tried to be helpful (7); and when only one of his legs was stiff (now they both are) so that he could move about on a bicycle, pedalling with his good leg while propping the other on the projecting front axle. (16)

Not until we read the novel's second part, of which Moran is the protagonist, do we gain deeper insight into Molloy's journey and come to understand its point of origin.

There we discover first of all that Moran lays hesitant claim to authorship of Molloy: "Perhaps I had invented him. I mean found him ready made in my head." (112) He even boasts of having invested his creature "with the air of a fabulous being, which something told me could not fail to help me later on." (111) "For who could have spoken to me of Molloy," he reflects, "if not myself and to whom if not myself could I have spoken of him?" (112) Moran thus insists on his authorial power to create characters, and see them in his mind's eye at places where neither he nor they can actually be, when he reflects: "For where Molloy could not be, nor Moran either for that matter, there Moran could bend over Molloy." (111) To find Molloy—as he is asked to do by his distant employer Youdi—and thereby bring him into being artistically, that is Moran's mission and obsession as a creative artist. As Anthony Hartley so acutely observes, in his *Spectator* article on Samuel Beckett, "Beckett's characters create and are created. That is their singularity."

His reflections in anticipation of the Molloy mission, reveal Moran is the artist wrestling with the task of creation in the manner of the hero setting out on a superhuman quest:

> It is lying down, in the warmth, in the gloom, that I best pierce the outer turmoil's veil, discern my quarry, sense what course to follow, find peace in another's ludicrous distress. Far from the world, its clamours, frenzies, bitterness and dingy light, I pass judgment on it and on those, like me, who are plunged in it beyond recall, and on him who has need of me to be delivered, who cannot deliver myself.

Moran is thus the hero as author who—in spite of his uneasiness and reluctance to set out on a mission which is a journey into the unknown, in spite of an awareness of his inadequacies and ignorance—must achieve the task of delivering the one who needs him. His artistic vision becomes his obsession, and he is well aware of the fact that, like any other hero, he is harnessed to a task which transcends himself as well as the object of his endeavor:

> "For what I was doing I was doing neither for Molloy, who mattered nothing to me, nor for myself, of whom I despaired, but on behalf of a cause which, while having need of us to be accomplished, was in its essence anonymous, and would subsist, haunting the minds of men, when its miserable artisans should be no more." (114f.)

The world as Moran conceives it, can be redeemed only through art; in proclaiming this, he aligns himself with philosophers like Nietzsche and writers like Proust.

In the novel's second part, we discover, moreover, that Molloy originated not merely as Moran's artistic vision, clamoring to be realized, but that he was known to Moran long before Youdi's call was heard by the artist hero. Molloy's name had echoed frequently, though indistinctly, in Moran's soul, "a first syllable, Mol, very clear, followed almost at once by a second, very thick, as though gobbled by the first, and which might have been oy as it might have been ose, or one, or even oc." (112) Indeed, Molloy had "come to" Moran at long intervals. (113) What makes Molloy different from Moran's earlier "clients" Murphy and Watt (actually the titular heroes of Beckett's previous novels), is the fact that he is more than a mission, that he is a part of Moran and sporadically asserts himself. It thus becomes apparent that we cannot presume to grasp the symbolic significance of the Molloy journey without first giving due consideration to Moran and his artistic quest, that the two are in fact inseparable.

Before he receives Youdi's message to search for Molloy, that is, before Molloy becomes his artistic obsession, Moran lives smug and satisfied among his possessions. The world which he shares with his son and his housekeeper is arranged sensibly and by the clock. His entire life is governed by will and reason and falls into an easy pattern of discipline and habit wherein formalized religion finds its natural place. To turn his son into a worthy member of this small, well-ordered universe, he rears him according to the bourgeois precept of *"sollst entbehren,"* a precept which once incited the creative genius of Goethe's Faust to rebellion.[1] The triviality of this existence, which

---

[1] Wolfgang von Goethe, *Faust I:*
Entbehren sollst du! sollst entbehren!
Das ist der ewige Gesang,

reposes primly on convention and habit, is revealed in a masterpiece of satire: Moran's conversation with the parish priest. Turning to the priest in a moment of profound anguish, Moran is unable to express this anguish and converses instead about his hen's loss of appetite. (101) For Moran has thus far excluded from his life all that is mysterious, incomprehensible, or irrational and admits that he finds it "painful . . . not to understand." (102)

To a man, "so meticulous and calm in the main, so patiently turned towards the outer world as towards the lesser evil, creature of his house, of his garden, of his few poor possessions . . . , reining back his thoughts within the limits of the calculable so great is his horror of fancy" (114) (thus Moran describes himself) Molloy appears as a chimera that haunts and possesses him. For Molly is his very opposite. Molloy "comes to" Moran and leaves an impression of utter absurdity. In his shapelessness and restlessness, he is a frightening creature, lacking all discipline, willpower and purposefulness. "He hastened incessantly on, as if in despair, towards extremely close objectives," Moran tells us. "Now, a prisoner, he hurled himself at I know not what narrow confines, and now, hunted, he sought refuge near the centre. He panted. He had only to rise up within me for me to be filled with panting." (113) Molloy's existence is totally detached from all that is accidental or useful and knows neither pattern nor reason. Whereas Moran is emphatically the individual living in time and space, a man "wrapped in the veil of Maya," in Schopenhauer's phrase, Molloy seems to be the unmolded, untamed essence of man: the stem *mol* (whose Latin meaning is *soft* or *pliable*) not pinned down by any precise suffix. Though mortal, he is timeless, ignoring the time-and-space-bound language of *homo sapiens*.

Molloy's "visitations" represent, undoubtedly, the stirrings within Moran of a subconscious, antithetical self. And each new assertion of that other self threatens Moran's accustomed world. It has in store for him change and suffering: "Then I was nothing but uproar, bulk, rage, suffocation, effort unceasing, frenzied and vain. Just the opposite of myself, in fact." (113) Thus Moran's quest for Molloy (who is a

Der jedem an die Ohren klingt,
Den unser ganzes Leben lang
Uns heiser jede Stunde singt.
. . . .
Der selbst die Ahnung jeder Lust
Mit eigensinnigem Krittel mindert,
Die Shöpfung meiner regen Brust
Mit tausend Lebensfratzen hindert.

secret part of himself) resembles the task which Yeats had set for each man, and the poet in particular: to seek out the "other self, the antiself or the antithetical self" and, indeed, to become—"of all things not impossible the most difficult"—that other self.[2] For as Moran advances upon his road into the Molloy country, he slowly changes into that other self and comes to resemble Molloy.

He becomes a restless wanderer detached from all that has been habit and formula in his life. The accidental is swept away. His family ties disintegrate. His son deserts him, and he no longer plays the part of the stern but loving father. When he returns to his house, his reliable housekeeper has disappeared from his life and with her the pattern of well-ordered existence. His certainties, his composure give way to doubt and insecurity. Even physically, a change takes place. His body begins to decay. One of his legs stiffens. He notices himself "a crumbling, a frenzied collapsing of all that has always protected me from all I was always condemned to be . . . it was like a kind of clawing towards a light and countenance I could not name, that I had once known and long denied." (148) Moran's journey is, therefore, not merely a departure from the confines of the familiar, not merely a metamorphosis. It represents a descent into his own subconscious where dwells Molloy—a *via dolorosa* into Molloy's immense universe of uncertainty and absurdity.

Already in 1931, while discussing Proust's Marcel of *Le temps retrouvé*, Beckett had described the artist's *via dolorosa,* from the vantage point of the critic:

> The old ego dies hard. Such as it was, a minister of dullness, it was also an agent of security. When it ceases to perform that second function, when it is opposed by a phenomenon that it cannot reduce to a condition of a comfortable and familiar concept, when, in a word, it betrays its trust as a screen to spare its victim the spectacle of reality, it disappears . . . with wailing and gnashing of teeth. The mortal microcosm cannot forgive the relative immortality of the macrocosm. (10)*

Like Proust's protagonist, Beckett's author-hero discovers his world of art in the "inaccessible dungeon of our being to which Habit does not possess the key" but where "is stored the essence of ourselves, the best of our many selves." (18) Unlike Marcel, however, Moran does not use

---

[2] Mercier, Vivian, "Yeats' *Mythologies*," *NYTBR* (2 August, 1959), VII, 4.
* [Grove Press ed., New York, n.d.]

involuntary memory as the occasional "diver" into that subconscious world of essences, but descends into it wholly to embrace there his antithesis and essence as man and as poet.

It is only appropriate that Beckett has cast the tale of this descent into the shape of ancient myths. For modern thinkers and writers, perhaps under the influence of Freud and Jung, have come to view the realm of myth as a reflection of the subconscious where is pooled the very essence of man. Thus the tale of Moran's journey is reminiscent of the myth of the "one hero in two aspects." Like this hero, Moran encounters innumerable obstacles on his way. His symbolic road towards Molloy is a series of trials. It is filled with mysterious encounters, with murder and deprivation. It occasions the rebellious departure of his son, on whom Moran had relied for companionship, filial devotion and ultimately guidance. Moran wanders in forlorn regions and dark forests, forever uncertain of his way, forever lonely. Joseph Campbell says of this "one hero in two aspects" that he ultimately "discovers and assimilates his opposite (his unsuspected self). . . . One by one the resistances are broken. He must put aside his pride, his virtue, beauty, and life, and bow or submit to the absolutely intolerable. Then he finds that he and his opposite are not different species but of one flesh." [3] They are, in Joyce's words, "equals of opposites, evolved by a onesame power of nature or of spirit, iste, as the sole condition and means of its himundher manifestation and polarised for reunion by the symphesis of their antipathies." [4]

Beckett's choice of "Molloy" as title for the entire novel reflects his insistence on the ultimate one-ness of Moran and Molloy in the manner of "the one hero in two aspects." Until we become aware of this underlying one-ness and the author-hero's development from Moran to Molloy, we remain puzzled by the fact that Moran, the apparent author-protagonist of the second part, is not accounted for in the title. In the light of their relationship, however, the novel's title brings to mind Beckett as the pseudo-philologist, the whimsical creator of such names as God-ot, Ma-g, Da-n, Ma-hood, and Mac-man, who might well maintain that, stripped of their uncertain suffixes, the roots *mor* and *mol* are identical—r and l being interchangeable liquids to the etymologist. In analogy to Moran's assimilation by Molloy, the syllable *mol*, with its suggestion of soft and unshaped matter,

[3] Campbell, Joseph, *The Hero with a Thousand Faces* (New York, 1949), 108.
[4] Joyce, James, *Finnegans Wake* (New York, 1939) p. 92, quoted by Campbell as a footnote to the preceding description.

was, of course, chosen to form the title in preference to the syllable *mor*.

In the light of this one-ness of Moran and Molloy resembling "the one hero in two aspects," we can begin to understand the significance of Molloy's journey. It must be seen as a continuation of the trek begun by Moran. As such, it represents an even further moving away from the realms of habit and will and a deeper penetration into that of essences, finding its symbolic culmination in the mother's room. There Molloy's artistic existence might be described in terms similar to those with which the critic Beckett evaluated that of Proust: "When the subject is exempt from will, the object is exempt from causality (Time and Space taken together). And this human vegetation is purified in the transcendental apperception that can capture the Model, the Idea, the Thing itself." (69)

We must not be misled by the novel's structure which seems to belie this assumption of a Moran-Molloy continuity. Obviously we encounter Molloy, hero-author of the first part, before we even are aware of Moran's existence and without in the least suspecting his provenance or the complex one-in-two relationship of the two protagonists. Because of their apparent independence from each other, the two parts of the novel leave us with an impression of incoherence. We are bewildered. Yet this bewilderment is easily disposed of, if we reverse the order of the two parts. Disregard for chronology should not surprise us in an author as obsessed with the absurdity of logic as is Beckett. Indeed, Beckett is quite aware of the liberty he takes with the organization of the novel and justifies it on artistic grounds. He claims that it is the messenger (that mysterious voice which induced Moran to leave his life of security and comfort and which guided both Moran and Molloy through the wilderness to their existence as writers) who urges Molloy to rearrange his story so that what was once the beginning is now nearly the end: "It was he told me I'd begun all wrong, that I should have begun differently. He must be right. I began at the beginning." (8) Thus is avoided that "vulgarity of a plausible concatenation," held in such contempt—so Beckett the critic had observed—by Proust and Dostoievski.

A reversal of the order in which the novel's parts are presented reveals, indeed, that the work would lose in artistic appeal what it would gain in clarity through such reorganization. If Moran's account of his adventures were to precede that of Molloy, the reader would be deprived of the element of suspense and the artistic challenge to pierce the mystery that shrouds their relationship, and with it the novel's meaning. The realization of the complex Moran-Molloy relationship —now the rich reward of the perceptive reader—would be reduced to something almost too obvious—that the author-hero Molloy continues the journey begun by the author-hero Moran. For Molloy's vague recollections of a past when he was sounder in mind and body and richer in human relationships coincide almost entirely with the facts we are told of Moran's life. Even the messenger, who urges Molloy to write, bears unmistakable resemblance to the messenger Gaber who played so vital a part in Moran's existence. Above all, Molloy's physical deterioration begins precisely at the stage where Moran's had ended. Deprived of the use of one leg, Moran dreamed of cleverly pedalling a bicycle with the help of his one good leg. Molloy, as we have seen, actually put into practice this manner of locomotion when he sets out on his adventures. At least this is what he recalls at a time when he has lost the use of both legs and is, indeed, deprived almost entirely of the services of his body and his senses.

Once the novel's first part is seen, however, in chronological sequence to the second part, this process of physical and sensorial deterioration, beginning with Moran's departure and increasing rapidly during Molloy's trek until he is reduced almost to bodilessness, begins to stand out as the novel's *leitmotif*. It must be seen as Beckett's symbolic restatement of an artistic truth he had recognized earlier when, as a critic, he extolled the "invisible reality" of Vinteuil's "little phrase," that Proustian symbol of the essence of art, as damning "the life of the body on earth as a pensum" and revealing "the meaning of the word: 'defunctus.' " (71–72) The destruction of the body and the senses is a further stripping away of all that is contingent in order to bare that which is essential. Thus Moran-become-Molloy, the antithetical self of his subconscious, proceeds even further on the road towards the core of artistic existence: his mother's room.

With its mythical overtones of rebirth and salvation, Molloy's quest is reminiscent of the traditional hero's road to the powerful "mother-destroyer" who is both mother and bride.[5] His mother never calls him son. She calls him Dan instead, which, when the n is dropped, means father—so he tells us. He calls her Mag, which, without the g, means mother. The image of his mother which thus hovers between Ma and Mag is also strangely fused with that of another woman in his life.

[5] Campbell, *op. cit.,* 121.

Although his mother is not presented as a symbol of beauty, youth, and virtue—quite the contrary in fact—Molloy says "Mother" in his hour of greatest need, as the medieval knight uttered the name of his beloved to guide him in distress. (87) Molloy's particular manner of arrival, his realization that, after having crawled through slush and darkness, he is in his mother's room, suggests a return to the womb and reminds us of the various myths of rebirth, the Dionysian mysteries as well as the Christian rite of baptism, whose mythical origin Campbell recalls.[6] Hence Beckett's evocation of the angelus at the beginning of Molloy's journey evoking the primary role of the Mother in the miracle of incarnation and as the instrument of salvation.

Yet Molloy, the hero as author in his quest of his mother, conjures up, above all, the poet's dreadful and difficult descent to the Mothers or Mothers of Being which Goethe presented in his *Faust*. Faust derives ultimate poetic knowledge from this descent to the very root and essence of things. Inspired by Goethe, the philosopher Nietzsche likewise considered arrival at the Mothers of Being as the ultimate to which the artist must aspire, though something to which he cannot attain without suffering. Nietzsche's conception of the manner of such attainment deserves, indeed, special mention because of its illuminating analogy with the Moran-Molloy dichotomy and fusion.

Nietzsche conceived of the world of art as the perpetual union and sundering of two elements: the Apollonian and the Dionysian. He saw the artistic world of Apollo as one of individual existence, a world concerned with reason and causality as well as measured beauty, but, by this very token, a superficial and sometimes empty world: the microcosm. He thought of the Dionysian world of art, on the other hand, as that of the macrocosm, where individual appearance is ephemeral, and birth and death are but brief manifestations in the endless ebb and flow of life. Such a world must appear absurd to the reasoning human being. However, in its very denial of the importance of individual existence and human rationality, it is nearer to the universal, the essence: ". . . by the mystical triumphant cry of Dionysus the spell of individuation is broken and the way lies open to the Mothers of Being (Faust II, Act 1), to the innermost heart of things." [7]

Nietzsche's esthetic antithesis provides a striking backdrop to the Moran-Molloy relationship as Beckett presents it: microcosm versus

---

[6] *Ibid.* 251.

[7] Nietzsche, Friedrich, "The Birth of Tragedy," *The Philosophy of Nietzsche* (New York, 1937), Modern Library Edition, Vol. I, 1033.

macrocosm as artistic concern. The Dionysian destruction of individuation has its counterpart in the deterioration of Molloy's body and his advance towards anonymity. Both see the ultimate end of art in its arrival at that "invisible reality" that Beckett admired in the music of Vinteuil's phrase. "A purely musical impression," as Proust had called it, "non-extensive, entirely original, irreducible to any other order of impression." (18) In Greek tragedy, so Nietzsche thought, the realm of Apollo was that of the *logos,* whereas the realm of Dionysus was that of music. Wherever the Dionysian predominates, art aspires to the universal, the immaterial. Beckett has, indeed, paid homage to the Dionysian element in art. For in *The Unnamable,* the last novel of the trilogy of which *Molloy* is the first, the realm of the immaterial is attained to such a degree that the nameless protagonist is "reduced to a disembodied voice, invaded and usurped upon by other voices," as Anthony Hartley put it so aptly.

This then is the Moran-Molloy journey as seen against the background of Nietzschean esthetics: a departure from the Apollonian and an arrival at the Dionysian element in art. It is not surprising, therefore, that Molloy, having virtually rid himself of his body and dwelling in his mother's room, lives in an immaterial world, a realm of essences, peopled with timeless creatures, detached from all that is tangible and accidental. His is a world without will, without causality, universal and nameless. From the pen of Moran there emerged a picture of people living within communities and, engaged in seemingly useful activity, communing with each other in everyday existence. His world was still filled with the individualized, tangible relationship of father and son, housekeeper and master, parish priest and parishioner, employer and agent. But the world of the writer-become-Molloy is the world of the macrocosm where individual existence shrinks into meaninglessness and human relations are reduced—or heightened—to the universal, the subconscious, the mythical.

In such a world Molloy has small belief in the power of language, the *logos,* to convey the essence of things:

. . . there could be no things but nameless things, no names but thingless names. I say that now, but after all what do I know about then, now when the icy words hail down upon me, the icy meanings, and the world dies too, foully named. All I know is what the words know, and the dead things, and that makes a handsome little sum, with a beginning, a middle, and an end as in the well-built phrase and the long sonata of the dead. (31)

Yet, in his mother's room, Molloy achieves at times that mystic union with the universe which Nietzsche considered the prerogative of the Dionysian artist and which, for Proust, in the form of music, embodied the highest achievement of art:

And there was another noise, that of my life become the life of this garden as it rode the earth of deeps and wildernesses. Yes, there were times when I forgot not only who I was, but what I was, forgot to be. Then I was no longer that sealed jar to which I owed my being so well preserved, but a wall gave way and I filled with roots and tame stems for example, stakes long since dead and ready for burning, the recess of night and the imminence of dawn, and then the labour of the planet rolling eager into winter, winter would rid it of these contemptible scabs. Or of that winter I was the precarious calm, the thaw of the snows which make no difference and all the horrors of it all all over again. (49)

Moran's escape from time, habit, and intelligence and his surrender to the Molloyan, the Dionysian element within him are to a certain degree paralleled in Beckett's own artistic development. More and more Beckett has found artistic fulfillment in the creation of a world without causality and will, the new-old world of myth and the subconscious. It is interesting that Beckett has referred to himself in specifically Nietzschean terms as a "non-knower," a "non-can-er" and claimed that "the other type of artist, the Apollonian, is absolutely foreign to me." [8] The author of the trilogy obviously sought and found himself an antithesis to the lucid Apollonian he proved himself in his essay on Proust. But Beckett recently confessed that *L'Innommable* landed him "in a situation that I can't extricate myself from." Perhaps we shall see, therefore, the Dionysian set out, in turn, in quest of the Apollonian.

[8] Shenker, Israel, "Moody Man of Letters," *NYTimes* (6 May, 1956), II, 1:6. In *The Birth of Tragedy*, Nietzsche refers to the great artist's ability as "Konnen," rendered in W. A. Haussmann's authorized translation as "can-ing." (London, 1910) p. 77.

Molloy

by Ludovic Janvier

One might characterize *Molloy* by these words: "hellish hope" (133), or again by these, a more detailed assassination: "Morning is the time to hide. They wake up, hale and hearty, their tongues hanging out for order, beauty and justice, baying for their due" (67), making the whole novel this killing-off of hope, or at least its gearing-down to a minimum by means of the expensive machinery of peaceful humor and lyric malice. Since Molloy travels, the Morans, father and son, travel too, the first searching his mother, the others in search of the first: and yet one must say immediately that this double wandering—as the two halves of the work separately testify—is pitiable, the route is impossible, and the traveler founders there almost totally. As for the journey's end, it is an ironic disappointment of the pilgrims' enterprise: Molloy seeks his mother's presence, but when he arrives she dies, she is dead; Moran rushes off after Molloy, but he misses him and will seek him unsuccessfully.

And yet such a view of the novel explains it imperfectly: it makes us, in our turn, fail to find that which in this superposition of two similar forms (the two voyages) and in the journey's cruelty indicates a journey by antiphrasis that is above all a measure of the self.

For this reason the characters' means of locomotion is in itself extremely expressive. Until now in Beckett's stories, whether it be Mercier and Camier, Watt, Murphy, or the hesitant shadows of the *Nouvelles,* the monad has traveled on foot. Now it risks a bicycle. Meanwhile, the step has grown heavy. Consequently, a clumsy earthling wishing to be an angel, Molloy at the beginning of his periplum bestrides a rather elementary bicycle that gives him many troubles but also the illusion of lightness and omnipotence. These troubles, we

"Molloy." *From* Pour Samuel Beckett *by Ludovic Janvier (Paris: Les Éditions de Minuit, 1966), pp. 48–61. Translated by J. D. O'Hara. Reprinted by permission of the publisher.*

recognize, are an undisguised punishment of fate: Molloy's bicycle embarrasses him whenever, walking beside it or settling his stiff leg on it, he wishes to go his way moderately, all the days of his life, through the midst of mankind. As for Moran, in the thick of his journey he decides to buy a bicycle that will compensate for his weakening body and allow him, with his son mounted behind, to fly efficaciously on what he believes to be Molloy's track. The bicycle, then, is an instrument of derisory super-power, of cheap super-lightness, to which the "hero" trusts his destiny: we have found Mercier and Camier with a bike, or rather evoking the memory of a bike, and their wanderings and tramplings retain the nostalgia of that former facility; we will find Hamm demanding—in the guise of a tranquilizer —two bicycle wheels; Nagg and Nell, his legless parents, recall their happiness on a bicycle built for two. . . . The body is powerless to continue, but it must continue: the bicycle is this impatience. The fall will be the harder: we will not be surprised to see this machine on which they have placed their hopes of soaring, or at least of departure and easy travel, escape them, lead them back to their initial state, and leave them even more infirm than before. Whether it be taken from them or abandon them, which is the case here, the bicycle betrays them, gravity weighs on the travelers, and the projected flight up bogs down. A mocked archangel, the pedestrian will know the property of speed no longer; worse, he will pick himself up with difficulty, or he will not recover at all. Leaving the house of his momentary protectress Lousse, where his bicycle escaped from him, Molloy moves along painfully on his crutches; and his speed will not cease to deteriorate, as elsewhere to a lesser degree but in an equally poignant manner Moran's speed will run down little by little: he will end his search hobbling toward his dilapidated house. Molloy will have had the more spectacular ambulatory fate: from the crutches that replaced the bicycle and that carry him with record slowness toward his goal, he passes to using accidents of the terrain—ditches, embankments, excavations, etc.—to propel himself along, all these modes ending in that reptation of which Molloy is the first example. "The black slush of leaves," he says, commenting on the change of his mode of travel, "slowed me down even more. But leaves or no leaves I would have abandoned erect motion, that of a man. And I still remember the day when, flat on my face by way of rest, in defiance of the rules, I suddenly cried, striking my brow, Christ, there's crawling, I never thought of that. . . . He who moves in this way, crawling on his belly, like a reptile, no sooner comes to rest than he begins to rest, and even the very movement is a kind of rest, compared to other movements, I mean those that have worn me out. And in this way I moved onward in the forest, slowly, but with a certain regularity, and I covered my fifteen paces, day in, day out, without killing myself." (89–90)

The humor cannot hide the essence of these words, bringing with them suddenly the Belacqua position, paradoxically, in the middle of Molloy's wandering search. Or rather, let us understand here that the wandering is tried and then condemned doubly in the light of that Belacqua truth that was Murphy's, but of which Murphy made a rather excessive use: "For it was not until his body was appeased that he could come alive in his mind." If the pilgrim comes clattering down from his bicycle, if he tottered even in the *Nouvelles,* and if, therefore, the traveler seeks a shelter in immobility and for his immobility, it's with the intention of giving himself up, all muscles relaxed, the body living for the final slackening of weight, for the pleasure of extended being and enclosed being. Since it's necessary to arrange the affair, to preserve this supination thanks to which the spirit returns to itself: it's Murphy's rocking chair, it's the canoe that carries the protagonist of "The End"; here it is the place from which Molloy and Moran speak to us at the end of their avatars and their fall: the peaceful and protected desk of the latter, the maternal room of the former, a place finally named for what it is, which Molloy inhabits to the point of making his own, one by one, all the objects that had belonged to her whom he "had to" rejoin. The end of the periplum is here: "In any case I have her room. I sleep in her bed. I piss and shit in her pot. I have taken her place. I must resemble her more and more" (7). And the identification reaches such a point, there is such an adherence to the calm womb, to the nourishing space of the room, that Molloy can for a moment become his own son, born peacefully from himself: "All I need now is a son. Perhaps I have one somewhere" (7). This much is clear: the voyage goes from the exterior to the interior: it leads to the center of the self.

Facing the world, whose presence suddenly imposes itself with more force, the monad feels its separation intensely. Other beings are only a single foil to it. We will therefore not be surprised that, in this double tale of travel and so apparently of movement out of the self, the outside doubly retreats and delegates each time as lures these creatures who always slip away before the quest that pursues them. Molloy searches for his mother. As we have seen, he finds her dying and has with her only derisory and cruel contacts whose disproportion is bursting with the tension, the dramatic necessity of his search. On the other hand, what stands out when, after settling down, Molloy tells us what brought him there, to his mother's home, is not only the solitude that is now his, but especially how much that solitude has been learned, has gone on growing: these parody *Wanderjahre* are the self's apprenticeship in its definitive limits. Whether it is a matter of the ridiculous police commissioner who raises before Molloy the insuperable barriers of decency, or of Lousse, his protectress, or of the women in charge of his amorous education, or of the silent shepherd with the herd he desires to join but which leaves when he approaches: they are so many dead ends and shut doors, sending him back to himself and making Molloy's essential goal, his mother, clear for what she is: an image of that re-ascent into one's self that the character desires and to which he is invited/forced by the attitude of mankind.

Moran has a son. He seeks Molloy first accompanied, then abandoned by that son. But whichever relationship one considers, to Molloy or his son, it appears that Moran is never more alone than in this accompaniment or this search, which nevertheless draws him out of himself. With his son, it is the era of the look. He fears the gaze of that being who resembles him to the point of bearing his first name, because he fears being surprised in his selfhood, whether masturbating—another image of menaced solitude—or simply living. He responds to this menace by making his offspring feel the weight of an authority that preserves itself by this morbid force. Seen through and through, Moran needs to see in his turn if he is not to be driven from his self; he must do evil in order to sense his own existence, and when he is reassured he is capable of a kind of moving tenderness: he is touched by that landscape that *The Unnamable* will call "the elms in se." But naturally it is in his tension toward Molloy that Moran feels most spectacularly the experience of imprisonment: one cannot avoid characterizing this real laceration in the calm of the only terms that make it legible: an immanence named Moran misses a transcendence named Molloy, and doing this shows that he is himself that transcendence he aimed for. To the extent that Moran advances, Molloy recedes; Moran is therefore his own horizon; and when his son finally abandons him, stripping him of his bicycle, it is so that he will be alone to seek in himself the Molloy he will become.

Let us enter into specifics. Two superposed adventures, which move in the same direction. How do they do it? Why two stories?

The superposition takes place, one suspects, otherwise than through this parity of intention, of tension. It is aided by traces and signs that seem *shared* by these two worlds. Here and there these signs have been tallied up, perhaps without complete recognition of whither the resemblance and communality tend and where they end.

The two bodies are brothers. We have seen that they suffer from the same progressive disabling; a notable detail of their kinship is that neither, in describing his sufferings, can recall on which side they occurred. Molloy confides to his report, speaking of his troubles with his foot: "But do you as much as know what foot we're talking about? No. Nor I" (80). This matches exactly two statements by Moran: falling asleep, he wonders if the knee that troubles him is the same as previously; awakening, he reflects: "I am still talking about my knee. But was it the same one that had waked me early in the night? I could not have sworn it was" (139). When Moran has only his incisors left (his son also has trouble with his teeth), Molloy is sucking his food and asking: "with what would I have chewed?" (54). When Molloy says that his hearing is still fine despite his age, Moran notes triumphantly: "I have an extremely sensitive ear" (129). The two characters confuse the same colors, in a striking manner. Are the clothes that Moran's son should wear for his departure blue or green? Moran doesn't know. Molloy has the same trouble: "For there reigned a kind of blue gloom, more than sufficient for my visual needs. I was astonished this gloom was not green, rather than blue, but I saw it blue and perhaps it was" (83). A final common detail speaks for itself: Moran, urging himself toward two-wheeled locomotion, says: "I trembled for my testicles which swing a little low" (157), which echoes Molloy's rather more detailed meditation on the same subject: "such testicles as mine, dangling at mid-thigh at the end of a meagre cord . . . accused me of having made a balls of it . . . the right lower than the left, or inversely, I forget, decaying circus clowns" (35f.). The two bodies, then, are similar, Molloy's taking the lead in the disintegration that leads them both toward the same posture—recumbent. We recall Molloy's satisfaction in being finally down, in being able to advance while lying down; Moran, too, rejoices only in the hope of total immobility. Molloy speaks, at different times, of stretching out despite the laws; Moran notes, during the harsh winter through which he travels: "Anyone else would have lain down in the snow" (165).

As for the "scenery," the space beyond that in which the two characters write of their travels, it is of the kind that a mirror divides and rejoins, opposing and reorienting it in two images reflecting each other. True, Molloy will deny that his home town is located on the coast, while Moran will locate it there; Molloy can only say that its name certainly begins with B, while Moran will specify that this Molloy he's been told to find lives in Bally. It is noticeable that for both men the garden plays an important role, whether it be that of Lousse where Molloy spent long hours, preferring it to the house, or that well-kept garden where Moran often sits, where he is surprised by the order to undertake his inquiry, and where he enjoys—not without affectation— the perfume of his flowers and the timeless dance of his bees. The same country of pastures, peat bogs, and thickets serves as setting for the travelers, who are also both involved with that forest in which the encounters occur and which they go through with that Cartesian persistence that makes souls strong, that forest that is also the testing ground whose duplication only helps to reveal the Dantean archetype:

> Nel mezzo del cammin di nostra vita
> mi ritrovai per una selva oscura,
> ché la diritta via era smarrita.
> [Halfway through life's journey
> I found myself within a dark forest
> in which the straight path grew lost.]

Finally, there is the similarity of some strange encounters to convince us of an unequivocal doubling of narrative time and space on themselves.

Moran and Molloy both accost a shepherd. Moran finds him in the evening, at nightfall. Molloy, who sleeps mornings, meets him on awakening. If this inversion is connected to the fact of their facing life with opposed attitudes, Moran continually leaving while Molloy tries only to return, so that altogether they turn their backs to each other in that mirror placed at the center, then this figure of the shepherd is that of an identity as well as a disparity. For instance, in both cases the sheep are black, and both characters try, with embarrassed speech or awkward gestures, to be accepted into an apparently paradisal society that attracts them as strongly as it strikes the reader. The narrative, then, twice is suspended in the same cautious silence, in the same ironic miracle affected by that presence of which Moran says: "How I would love to dwell upon him" (158), while Molloy says: ". . . and space with its sounds again, and the shepherd watching me sleep and under whose eyes I opened my eyes" (28). Without succumbing to the facility of a biblical reference, we may still understand that the soft Molloy wishes to be a sheep in the care of that father whose gaze enriches—but in vain. On the other hand, the hard Moran senses himself guilty—he admits it freely—of looking like a butcher in the middle of that flock whose pastor recalls the son who will soon leave him. Both sides of the same situation, with each character sensing a tenderness that eludes him.

Moran and Molloy are the executioners of a man encountered in the forest. Someone who is not dissimilar to Molloy throws himself at him and asks Molloy to share his hut. A charcoal-burner, perhaps. Molloy feels menaced in his helotism and leaves him for dead after felling him with blows from his crutches and his heels. A man comes toward Moran, resembling him amazingly—"same little abortive moustache, same little ferrety eyes, same paraphimosis of the nose" (151)—and imposes himself on Moran in Moran's own style, authoritarian, demanding, while Molloy's visitor imitated rather well his partner's manner, innocent and persuasive. Moran kills him with the same disordered industry that he might display in attacking his double.

Both Moran's path and Molloy's cross that of an old man we may designate as the man with the stick.

This individual, whom Molloy evokes at the beginning of his story and who passes before him without seeing him, is part of a pair of strollers, A and C (one thinks immediately of Mercier and Camier), before being found alone on our hero's path and indicating to him, despite his costume, the nobility of his style and the dignity of being a man and alone. He leans on a sturdy stick. But this character recalls not only Mercier, he recalls also that crazed being who, in "The Calmant," runs in all directions through the city, looking around at the lights and the passersby without understanding anything, and who, among other bizarre acts, climbs rapidly up the winding stair of a church steeple, from which he dominates the landscape: all of which is specifically evoked here when Molloy invents for this stroller a probable past. He is more than a fabulous brother of former characters, however; he is Molloy's brother; he is also Moran's, since like him he carries a cigar and wears a hat held under the chin by an elastic or a tight string. But Moran also, in his turn, meets the old man. Leaning on a heavy stick like a club, he is ageless, and his face is dirty, handsome, and hairy. Prowling around Moran's camp, he ends by asking for a morsel of bread in a voice that has lost the use of speech. Moran asks to see and to touch the stick; he takes it in his hand for a moment and returns it. The other leaves. Afterwards, Moran cannot rest until he also has a stick to lean on. Since he has no knife, however, he must use his umbrella as a stick.

What, then, is the relationship between Moran and Molloy? What this appearance of identity and this superposition of anecdotes reveal to us is the sharing, by these two ambiguous forms, of a common *space*. The novel can therefore look to us like a playing card printed with a double figure composed of two similar and antithetical—but never contradictory—halves. Two names for the same face.

The space is certainly common to both. But what about the time?

> That a man like me, so meticulous and calm in the main, so patiently turned toward the outer world as towards the lesser evil, creature of his house, of his garden, of his few poor possessions, discharging faithfully and ably a revolting function, reining back his thoughts within the limits of the calculable so great is his horror of fancy, that a man so contrived, for I was a contrivance, should let himself be haunted and possessed by chimeras, this ought to have seemed strange to me and been a warning to me to have a care, in my own interest. (114)

So says Moran when, in that long interrogation in which he speaks of Molloy, he takes the bearings of his subject and tries to illuminate in it whatever yields to his familiarity. The words in it that relate to Molloy have a very lively power to upset; they designate a desire, a need at least as great as that obedience to orders which, one knows, will send Moran on his vain search. "Then I was nothing," says he of those moments when Molloy "visits" him, "but uproar, bulk, rage, suffocation, effort unceasing, frenzied and vain. Just the opposite of myself, in fact. It was a change. . . . I saw him disappear, his whole body a vociferation. . . ." (113) Molloy in Moran is therefore a fate physically undergone, the quest, and physically experienced, sorrow. In Moran the scene of the drama abruptly identifies itself as Molloy: "He panted. He had only to rise up within me for me to be filled with panting" (113). Even more, he is at the center, he is the being who, in Moran, takes on Moran's form, becomes the one who "now, a prisoner, . . . hurled himself at I know not what narrow confines, and now, hunted, . . . sought refuge near the centre" (113), an idea expressed earlier in "there where Molloy could not be, nor Moran either for that matter" (111), and especially in that hasty comment, thrown off negligently but stating strongly the superposition and even the conjunction: "A natural end [for Molloy] seemed unlikely to me, I don't know why. But then my own natural end, and I was resolved to have no other, would it not at the same time be his?" (113f.)

To the extent, then, that he sheds his self and is set in order, that is to say in disorder, in "the inennarrable contraption" (114) that is his life, Moran then *reveals* Molloy and approaches him. When he returns home without having found him, one now knows why he is ready to go about on crutches: it was on crutches that Molloy set out. Moran's time and Molloy's time, for the reader, have in common the characteristic of measuring each about a year, between the two summer solstices. But this round-trip time is measureable only with reference to the traveler who lives it: and Molloy's time is oriented toward an arrival, an end painfully attained, which makes for a slow passage of time; while Moran's time is an accelerated time in which everything happens precipitately, is telescoped, moves at high speed toward a goal. Molloy never finishes arriving; Moran constantly leaves: in Moran's leaving is Molloy's arrival:

> And on myself too I pored, on me so changed from what I was. And I seemed to see myself ageing as swiftly as a day-fly. But the idea of ageing was not exactly the one which offered itself to me. And what I saw was more like a crumbling, a frenzied collapsing of all that had always protected me from all I was always condemned to be. Or it was like a kind of clawing towards a light and countenance I could not name, that I had once known and long denied. (148)

At this point we must recall that we have undoubtedly assisted at one of the symbolic deaths experienced by Moran: when he met in the forest that man in the blue serge suit, in whom it had not been difficult to see his double, it had been to kill him. His narrative, then, insisted not only on the resemblance, but also on the strange relief and the renewed astonishment that seized the criminal: he feels light; for a while his legs carry him better as those of the corpse stiffen; he cannot find the felt hat his victim wore, but on the other hand he retrieves from the ground not far from the body the straw hat that he thought had stayed on his head. This encounter must have been the occasion of one of those rebirths through which Moran was able to give himself up completely to the hastening of the transformation—Molloy. Moran's time, then, precedes Molloy's; or rather, Moran and Molloy are two consecutive moments of a single process of becoming.

Not yet convinced? Molloy's age is canonic. One day he speaks of himself as seeing "a young old man" (62), which gives him a feeling of calm superiority. Moreover, he describes his age as "enormous." Further on, he will speak of his "astonishing old age" (82). Moreover, he has a past that seems to contain, very distantly, Moran's past, but not the other way around. It is Molloy who speaks of having had, undoubtedly long ago, a son and a "chambermaid" whom he loved: except for the love, this is Moran . . .

What is the result of the process of becoming—this Molloy undiscoverable anywhere but in himself? A being who even has difficulty identifying himself. The reciprocal structure is not without irony here, demonstrating the resignation-annihilation that is the book's goal. With what pungency and what strange force the odyssey of Moran runs its course before the eyes of the spectator holding the book! Like the spectator of a tragedy who knows what will befall the hero and suffers in advance for him in his progressive ruin, the reader who measures the times and spaces leading toward each other sees, distanced by humor and pity, the birth-collapse of Moran joining the collapse-birth of Molloy, his appointed goal. The non-chronology of the novel serves to return us toward the beginning, knowing the next-to-last term,[1] the better to disclose what in existence ironically sums existence up. Furthermore —and this is perhaps the major reason—the anteposition of Molloy's failure with respect to Moran's search tells us *before all* that the end is never measurable nor known; that one is always reborn. Finally, we observe that Molloy's narrative is constructed in such a way that its beginning with reference to the order of the novel is its end with reference to the order of his journey; and Moran's is the same. It is when they have settled down, at the end of their periplum, that they can speak. In reading the novel, then, we do not move forward in the life of the two "authors," we go backwards. The story is written in reverse; in both cases we go toward the beginning. Considered separately each story, once completed, is a perpetual self-starting recommencement, since its end returns to its beginning. And the two stories, contradicting and confirming each other, have the same relationship. The Molloy story moves backwards toward the Moran story in unwinding itself, and the end of one throws us to the beginning of the other. The book is a spiral suggesting an endless ascent after a conclusive descent, and so on.[2] Such is

---

[1] "There is never a last, by the sea" (75), says Molloy, speaking of his visit.
[2] At one time Molloy says, "Then I resumed my spirals" (68).

the motivating force that depicts the journey of being, despite itself, toward the land of better knowledge.

Since, despite itself, there is such a force. It is called Gaber, and Moran presents him to us as sent by Youdi, his master, to persuade Moran to set out on Molloy's trail. We see him again near the middle of the story, when he gives Moran the order—again from Youdi—to return home; and finally we know that when Moran has reached his domain it is again by Gaber's orders that the report that constitutes Moran's story must be, is, has been undertaken. Gaber is always thirsty, and he comes on Sundays . . . A man who is always thirsty and visits Molloy on Sundays is also behind that story; his presence has the same persistence as that of Gaber; it is Gaber's.

The motivating force, then, is activated from on high; it is suspended in a space of which neither Molloy nor Moran is master. This Youdi God the father and this Gaber archangel Gabriel are the order that summons existence, as we see; they incarnate the utterance that leads us from the interior toward the horizon of our selves. It is certainly a matter of utterance, since—unlike the dark envoys of Kafka's castle— these "orders" force the character to tell tales about himself, to speak himself. It is by command that Molloy writes his tale, submitting his copy at each return of his visitor. Once he was asked to begin the tale again; this false start is perhaps not unrelated to Molloy's past (whether it be Moran or the "aberrations" of the Beckettian journey up to that point), and the character will recall it in adjusting his story here and there—"no, that won't work"—in order to yield more successfully to the necessities of the narrative, to submit to the inclination that leads to the center. The same dependence, the same readjustments are naturally experienced by Moran, to the point of that final contradiction: "It was not midnight. It was not raining," of the first words of his confession: "It is midnight. The rain is beating on the windows." In that contradiction we can see the extent to which the reality of events has no other basis than obedience to a discourse that, unsubmissive to the world, supersedes it.

Moreover, it is a voice that best represents Gaber when he is no longer there, that takes his role, that *is* Gaber. Molloy knows it and Moran too; each hears it repeatedly, and it speaks best in these words of Moran:

And the voice I listen to needs no Gaber to make it heard. For it is within me and exhorts me to continue to the end the faithful servant I have always been, of a cause that is not mine, and patiently fulfil in all its bitterness my calamitous part, as it was my will, when I had a will, that others should. And this with hatred in my heart, and scorn, of my master and his designs. (132)

We arrive then at the understanding that Molloy and Moran, and Gaber and Youdi, and this voice itself are supernumeraries in a game in which the ultimate existence of the self is risked. The perfection of this inexhaustible work, notably this astonishing structure that makes it as smooth and complete to the eye as a boulder and as unbreakable, its extratemporal recommencement, its allusive and nevertheless effective solidity, all that illustrates the labor of thought over itself, that anonymous labor[3] that is basically the difficult taking over of the spirit by the spirit, "that rumour rising at birth and even earlier" (10). With all this apparatus making it at once a novel of adventure and a mental landscape, *Molloy* is a metaphor[4] of the journey toward the self. Soon, immobile and straining itself to hear, being will turn towards its immediate future: words.

[3] "And even my sense of identity was wrapped in a namelessness often hard to penetrate" (31); and especially ". . . a cause which, while having need of us to be accomplished, was in its essence anonymous, and would subsist, haunting the minds of men, when its miserable artisans should be no more" (114 f.).

[4] Its essential form. Molloy is a myth; his present tense is the mythological present, as he says (26). The detour through fable in order to venture speaking of this return to the sources sufficiently indicates modesty before the enterprise. At the same time this backward movement, because it is epic, and this fable, because it is cumbersome, will always be with us. The fear of speaking causes this novel to strike one forcibly and will cause the writer to construct similar revelation-machines henceforth.

Malone "Given Birth To Into Death"

by John Fletcher

Unrepentant, I would still consider the second volume of the Trilogy to be "quite straightforward";[1] the fact that Penguin Books have chosen *Malone Dies* as a representative "Modern Classic" in their paperback series would seem to confirm this view. It has not attracted the critical attention which has been focussed on the psychological complexities of *Molloy* or on the experimental daring of *The Unnamable*. To return to the subject again, however, is tacitly to admit that all has not been said; I should like now to delve more deeply into the notion of death, which, it seems to me, is central to the novel. What does it mean "to die"? When do we cease from living and enter the state of death? These are the questions with which Beckett has wrestled elsewhere (notably in the poem that meditates on "these long shifting thresholds," [2] written at about the same time as *Malone Dies*) and which, in an age of heart-transplants, give us all matter for reflection.

A central uncertainty, in fact, surrounds the moment when Malone "legally" dies. This can be placed some pages before the end of the novel, making the sanatorium a hell (cf. the inmates' cloaks, like those of Dante's hypocrites),[3] or earlier, or later: there is no lack of ambiguous indications, any of which may be taken at their face value. But a careful count reveals a majority of assertions from Malone which point clearly to the fact that he dies as the pencil falls from his hand at the very end: the frenzy of the closing pages is therefore not so much infernal as the result of his death-agony. "Throes are the only trouble,"

[1] *The Novels of Samuel Beckett* (London: Chatto and Windus, 1964), p. 151.
[2] *Poems in English* (New York: Grove Press, 1963), p. 57.
[3] As J. D. O'Hara surmises, in a letter to me.

he asserts, "I must be on my guard against throes" (179)—but throes, according to the Oxford dictionary, can mean birth-pangs as well as death-pains. We are thus brought to the core of Malone's thinking, that death is a second birth, a birth into a state that remains unknown and unknowable, but fascinating and terrifying at the same time.

His first striking statement of this theme is the following:

> My eyes, I shall open my eyes, look at the little heap of my possessions, give my body the old orders I know it cannot obey, turn to my spirit gone to rack and ruin, spoil my agony the better to live it out, far already from the world that parts at last its labia and lets me go. (189)

Later on he thinks of himself as "an old foetus" who has rotted his mother, so that "she'll drop me with the help of gangrene, . . . I'll land headforemost mewling in the charnel-house" (225). Later still, as the end approaches, he feels the rhythm of travail acting on him:

> And I? Indubitably going, that's all that matters. Whence this assurance? Try and think, I can't. Grandiose suffering. I am swelling. What if I should burst? The ceiling rises and falls, rises and falls, rhythmically, as when I was a foetus. Also to be mentioned a noise of rushing water, phenomenon *mutatis mutandis* perhaps analogous to that of the mirage, in the desert. The window. I shall not see it again. Why? Because, to my grief, I cannot turn my head. Leaden light again, thick, eddying, riddled with little tunnels through to brightness, perhaps I should say air, suck-ing air. All is ready. Except me. I am being given, if I may venture the expression, birth to into death, such is my impression. The feet are clear already, of the great cunt of existence. Favourable presentation I trust. My head will be the last to die. Haul in your hands. I can't. The render rent. My story ended I'll be living yet. Promising lag. That is the end of me. I shall say I no more. (283)

This is, to put it mildly, an odd conception of death. To understand it, we must look elsewhere in Beckett's writings. The womb is every-where seen as a place of protective calm (how frequently the words "calm"—"cawm" to Estragon—and "calmative" crop up in Beckett's works). Belacqua "wants very much to be back in the caul" where one is spared "night sweats." Murphy refuses to wear a hat, "the memories it awoke of the caul were too poignant," and the padded cells of the Magdalen Mental Mercyseat appeal to him profoundly as a substitute for the womb, which he, like Malone, was foolish enough to have "con-sented to leave" (240). Mahood curses his mother for having ejected him into the world (323). Life is everywhere seen as a punishment, a

"pensum" for what is called in *Proust* "the sin of having been born,"
and mothers are ambiguous figures: Molloy's is a disgusting old crone
(19), Moran's is probably Martha,[4] and Malone's is perhaps the old
woman whom he believes to be even older than he is and who ministers
to his needs (185) until her own demise precipitates his by cutting off
his supply of soup. By the same token, fathers are tyrant-figures, hated
and feared, from Watt's Mr Knott onwards. Molloy is terrorised by the
man who collects his manuscript pages, Moran by Youdi, Malone by
the sinister visitor in the bowler-hat, and the Unnamable by his anonymous tormentors.

Nostalgia for the womb; ambiguous attitude, one compounded of
love (cf. "I suck," [199]) and detestation, for the mother who ejected the
hero from the womb; and dread and loathing felt for the father, who is
obscurely felt to have been ultimately responsible for the expulsion
(cf. that strange short story, *The Expelled*): these are the dominant
sentiments of Beckettian man. They enable us to understand Malone's
attitude to death.

For we can now see why he sees death as a second, and perhaps hap-
pier birth. Death will finally reverse the process that has been so painful
to recall, and for which life itself has not been sufficient to atone. Malone, dying at last, is "content, necessarily" (179), for the "old debtor"
is about to repay him for his long and dolorous existence (180). While
waiting for this long-overdue settlement, he decides to tell himself
"stories": but, despite his oratorical precautions, it is clear that he is
telling his own story, that he is, in fact, succumbing to autobiography.
("I wonder if I am not talking yet again about myself," [189]). The novel
thus has a "very pretty" completeness: "on the threshold of being no
more I succeed in being another" (194), but "another" who is but an
improved (that is, fictionalised) version of himself. The drowning man
sees his life again, in a flash; Malone has a little more time, but only so
long as his body metabolises the remains of that soup, and his pencil-
lead lasts out. "Then it will be all over with the Murphys, Merciers,
Molloys, Morans and Malones, unless it goes on beyond the grave"
(236). As the end approaches, Malone no longer has the time to indulge
in "mere" literature: "When it rained, when it snowed. On" (280). He
finally summons just enough strength to clear the decks, rapidly and
savagely, condemning his creatures to drift out to sea (a figure of the
womb) to meet the fate of the hero of another story, *The End*. He has

[4] As I argue in "Interpreting *Molloy*," *Samuel Beckett Now*, ed. M. J. Friedman
(Chicago: University of Chicago Press, 1970).

killed them off symbolically with his pencil, as Lemuel had slaughtered the sailors with his hatchet (288).

Behind Malone stands Samuel Beckett, who writes similarly in an exercise-book (209), or so the catalogers of his manuscripts inform us, hoping no doubt with Malone that "this [will] be my last journey, down the long familiar galleries" (236). The narrator, like the rest, is an ambiguous figure in this novel: "the iron gates clashing and dragging at their posts" (206) is Samuel's personal reminiscence, as is much else besides.[5] This novel is therefore not only concerned with life and death, but with the crisis of identity, and beyond that, it manifests the ambiguity of narrational point of view which we have come to associate with post-Proustian fiction. For who is Malone, but simultaneously the creator, and avatar, of Murphy, Molloy, Moran, and the others? And what is this book, but the projection and exorcism of private traumas, and their sublimation into art? In other words, *Malone Dies* represents a painful—but ultimately successful—"birth into literature" both for its moribund narrator and for its surviving author.

"Undoubtedly," writes Erich Fromm, "if the infant could think at the moment of the severance of the umbilical cord, he would experience the fear of dying"—

> At any new step, at any new stage of our birth, we are afraid again. We are never free from two conflicting tendencies: one to emerge from the womb, from the animal form of existence into a more human existence, from bondage to freedom; another, to return to the womb, to nature, to certainty and security. In the history of the individual, and of the race, the progressive tendency has proven to be stronger, yet the phenomena of mental illness and the regression of the human race to positions apparently relinquished generations ago, show the intense struggle which accompanies each new act of birth.[6]

Not only mental illness, Mr. Fromm: works of art, too, can "show the intense struggle which accompanies each new act of birth." And in an elevated position in the hierarchy of such profoundly necessary works of art ranks *Malone Dies*. "It's vague, life and death" (225). Man, according to Georges Bataille, is the only creature who spends his life mythologising his death: the second novel of Beckett's Trilogy must surely, then, be reckoned one of his most sustained, and perverse, attempts at doing so.

---

[5] See *The Novels of Samuel Beckett*, pp. 159 and 175–76.
[6] *The Sane Society* (London: Routledge and Kegan Paul, 1956), p. 27.

About Structure in *Malone Dies*

by J. D. O'Hara

I should like to begin by borrowing Lemuel's hatchet and hacking my subject into pieces, distinguishing the structure of *Malone Dies* from structures within *Malone Dies*. There are, for example, many narrative elements in the novel. Malone's dying is an obvious one. With increasing frequency toward the end of the novel we hear about alterations in space, time, sound, light, and temperature. If we are symbolically inclined we may seek occult meaning in all this, but we surely agree that these alterations are basically to be understood as constituting one of the threads of plot; they are all symptomatic of Malone's approaching death. The same is true of the inventory, the visitor, Malone's plans and memories, the loss of stick and pencil; all these narrative elements are individually clear and recognizable structures. They are the kinds of equipment with which any conventional novelist might construct a novel, but in *Malone Dies* they do not constitute the structure. Additionally, the novel contains many examples of what T. J. Roberts calls microworks: nearly or completely self-contained wholes within the novel. The stories of Sapo-Macmann and the Lamberts fit into this category, and even smaller examples may be isolated. The scene (210f.)[1] in which Adrian Saposcat discusses the gift pen with his wife, for instance, is a marvelous set piece à la Sterne, and we may take the story of Moll and Macmann from its context and consider it separately. But these narrative elements and microworks are to the novel's structure as bricks to a building, and my topic is not the bricks but the blueprints.

[1] The text for all references to the trilogy is Samuel Beckett, *Three Novels by Samuel Beckett: Molloy, Malone Dies, The Unnamable* (New York: Grove Press, 1965).

Most of Beckett's critics have noticed the Cartesian ideas pervading his works and have stressed the idea of duality, especially with regard to the mind-body relationship. It is a topic for explicit comment by the characters throughout the early works. In *More Pricks Than Kicks,* for instance, Belacqua Shuah "scoffed at the idea of a sequitur from his body to his mind"; in *Murphy* most of the characters comment on the topic; and in *Watt* it is extensively supplemented by the subject-object duality. As the canon progresses, Beckett naturally tires of the topic, but it becomes increasingly important; the characters have less and less to say about it, but the structure of the later works is increasingly characterized by it. In the stories of *More Pricks Than Kicks* duality is not a consistent structural element. One might speak of duality in *Murphy,* opposing Murphy's world to that of the other characters, but the division would be arbitrary; no one world contains the clowns and Celia and the inhabitants of the Magdalen Mental Mercyseat. Nor can *Watt* be divided satisfactorily between Watt and Knott or Watt and Sam. The first serious use of structural duality probably occurs in the abandoned novel *Mercier et Camier,* although those who have read it reach no agreement on the sense or significance behind the double hero.

But with the trilogy (itself originally projected as a double work[2]) duality establishes itself as an integral part of structure. Everyone notices the deliberate split of *Molloy* into two parts quite separate and distinct, though tantalizingly on the verge of fitting together, and John Fletcher has suggested that the Morans, father and son, echo the earlier pseudocouple Mercier and Camier. But there is more to be said.

After a two-day search for his dropped pencil Malone tells us that those days have "brought me the solution and conclusion of the whole sorry business, I mean the business of Malone (since that is what I am called now) and of the other. . . . And it was, though more unutterable, like the crumbling away of two little heaps of finest sand, or dust, or ashes, of unequal size, but diminishing together as it were in ratio, . . . and leaving behind them, each in its own stead, the blessedness of absence" (222).

The image of the heaps is ironic; in a short time Malone will speak of Zeno's heaps of millet (225), and we'll realize that two heaps diminishing in ratio can never achieve "the blessedness of absence." There is additionally Malone's vision of a malicious creator who will repile the sand and start the process over (224). But the most curious thing about

---

[2] John Fletcher, *The Novels of Samuel Beckett* (New York: Barnes & Noble, 1964), p. 129.

the image is that it is of *two* heaps, apparently representing Malone and "the other." We may guess that the heaps represent Malone and Sapo—both crumbling, but Sapo more quickly since his life is compressed into the smaller heap.

These unequal heaps represent "the solution and conclusion of the whole sorry business," which at present is Malone's business but previously was the business of *Molloy*. Although the disproportion between Molloy and Moran is scarcely noticeable (84 pp. *vs.* 83⅓), Moran's crumbling, like Sapo's, is both briefer and more accelerated than Molloy's. The two heaps, then, remind us not only that disintegration is a repeated element of structure in the two novels, but that it is a dual collapse in both cases. In *Molloy* the duality is embodied in distinct and vaguely related characters. It begins to become internal in *Malone Dies,* where one of the characters is created by the other; and it reaches its goal in *The Unnamable,* where Mahood and the Unnamable are dual and simultaneous aspects of the same identity—still crumbling, still progressively diminishing toward the unreachable absence.

In *Malone Dies,* then, duality (and disintegration) is at once a theme and a structural device. Critics see it as dividing the characters into creator and creatures and the novel into reality and fiction; and many other divisions are suggested: fact and imagination, passive and active existence, operator and puppet, etc. None of these divisions is finally satisfactory. If we attempt to look at the novel as a whole, we are put off, here as with *Molloy,* by its obvious two-sidedness; but if we attempt to define this two-sidedness we realize that it can never be clearly perceived—partly because the terms on each side elude definition and partly because they are not completely separable. Let us consider some of them.

The creator-creature division is among the most obvious, since Malone quite explicitly tells us that he is a writer and that he is telling a story about Sapo. But Malone the creator is not separable from the other side of the division. He is also a creation; the author of *Malone Dies* is Beckett, not Malone. Furthermore, Malone eludes definition; he is neither a coherent nor a self-contained term. He refers to himself as "having been nothing but a series or rather a succession of local phenomena all my life, without any result" (234), and we know him only as a succession of moods and assertions. In any practical sense we know almost nothing about him, and what he asserts about his past, his present, and his intentions for the future is almost always put in doubt or contradicted by another assertion or by circumstances beyond his control. "Malone" is simply "what I am called now" and no aid to identity; we never learn who calls him by that name, if indeed anyone does.

His links to *Molloy* are innumerable and unsatisfactory. It is tempting to say that he was once Molloy, since he emphasizes his possession of a room in which he regained consciousness, having lost it elsewhere (183), and he thinks that "perhaps I came in for the room on the death of whoever was in it before me" (182). Actually we left Molloy in two places—in his mother's room, where he was writing his story, and on the edge of a forest, where his story abruptly ends. Malone came to consciousness in a room, but he also vaguely recalls a forest: "Perhaps I was stunned with a blow, on the head, in a forest perhaps, yes, now that I speak of a forest I vaguely remember a forest" (183). But neither of the two men stunned and probably killed by a blow on the head in a forest can be identified as Molloy. He himself kills someone who seems to be a charcoal burner (84f.), and Moran kills someone much like himself (150f.). Among Malone's possessions is a club (249) that links him to the character Molloy calls C (10–13, 145–47). But the club is stained with blood, suggesting that in the past Malone was a stunner as well as one stunned. He is linked to Molloy by such relics as a bicycle bell and half a crutch (252); he loves to suck (199, 222), which reminds us of Molloy's sucking stones; and he speaks of a previous existence by the sea (225f.), but we cannot—to cut a dull investigation short—we cannot say definitely that Malone was once Molloy or anyone else. We can only say that he has a prehistory that puts him in some relation not only to *Molloy* but to the whole Beckett canon: when he dies, he tells us, "it will be all over with the Murphys, Merciers, Molloys, Morans and Malones, unless it goes on beyond the grave" (236).

Every reader notices the signs telling us that Malone is inventing Sapo's story as he goes along, e.g., "Sapo had no friends—no, that won't do" (189); but few notice that the same signs are present when he speaks of himself. "When my chamber-pot is full I put it on the table, beside the dish," he tells us. "Then I go twenty-four hours without a pot. No, I have two pots" (185). In the same place he tells us how he communicated with the woman tending him, but then concludes, "All that must be half imagination" (185).

His creation Sapo is equally evasive. Malone begins by insisting on Sapo as an escape from himself. "Nothing is less like me than this patient, reasonable child," he says, and therefore writing about Sapo will enable him, before he dies, to "frolic, ashore, in the brave company I have always longed for, always searched for, and which would never have me" (193). But soon he speaks of Sapo as "that child I might have been, why not?" (208), and finally he abandons the pretense of escaping from himself: "I shall try and make a little creature, to hold in my arms, a little creature in my image, no matter what I say. And seeing what a poor thing I have made, or how like myself, I shall eat it" (226). Malone is trying to play; Sapo's father says "he ought to play more games" (193); Moll cares for Macmann as an old woman cares for Malone; the daily routine at Saint John of God's resembles that where Malone lives; Malone and Sapo both like arithmetic dealing with things (186f., 201), etc. In short, the separation of creator and creation cannot be maintained.[3]

But we cannot go to the other extreme and speak of Sapo as merely a fictional Malone. Malone distributes his knowledge and qualities rather indiscriminately throughout his stories. Speaking of his room, he says that "the light is against my window, but it does not come through" (220); earlier he had attributed the same effect to sunlight on the Lamberts' cottage (203). He gives his childhood near the stonecutters to Lemuel (206f., 286), with whom he identifies himself at the novel's end. But most curious of all—and Malone shares our curiosity—are Sapo's eyes, which resemble those of a gull. As Fletcher delicately suggests, and as photographs of Beckett suggest, those are Beckett's own eyes. (They also appear elsewhere in his fiction.) There are other autobiographical elements as well: the stonecutters come from Beckett's childhood, for instance, and the Lamberts from his enforced stay in the Vaucluse during the war. The eyes are somehow of a different order, however. They make us conscious of Sapo as created not only by Malone and Beckett but also out of Malone and Beckett. One final oddity: Moran owns a silver kniferest (115) and Molloy steals one, not knowing what it is, from Lousse (63). The next time we hear of it (one tends, reading Beckett, to assume that his stage props are used over and over again) it is among Macmann's possessions, having traveled, like Sapo's eyes, from one order of reality to another.

The creator-creature duality, then, holds good only so long as we speak of it in general terms; when we examine it closely, all sorts of difficulties arise. The other dualities are equally fragile. We cannot speak of reality and fiction without pretending that Malone is real,

---

[3] Cf. Molloy's complaint: "Saying is inventing. Wrong, very rightly wrong. You invent nothing, you think you are inventing, you think you are escaping, and all you do is stammer out your lesson, the remnants of a pensum one day got by heart and long forgotten . . ." (32).

which would be silly. (Certainly Malone would think it so.) We can hardly consider Malone as Sapo's puppet-master. Though at times he is in charge, as when he gives Sapo friends and when he renames him, he is more often bothered by his lack of knowledge about Sapo and by his inability to understand him. Malone loses him and finds him, as if Sapo had an existence independent of his creator's will, and he is unable to kill Sapo off, despite his repeated wish to do so. At the end it is Malone who dies, while Sapo and his fellow inmates drift unharmed forever beneath the impotent menace of Lemuel's raised hatchet-pencil. What Beckett said about Sapo, Malone might equally have said: "He got a bit out of hand" (Fletcher, *Novels,* p. 175).

In arguing that these dualities are imprecise I do not intend to undermine my assertion that duality is a primary element of structure in *Malone Dies*; I simply wish to indicate that it is of a particular kind here and carries a particular sense. One way of suggesting this sense is to recall an early remark by Malone. Speculating on the stories he plans to tell, he says, "Perhaps I shall not have time to finish. On the other hand perhaps I shall finish too soon. There I am back at my old aporetics. Is that the word? I don't know" (181). It is surely no accident that *The Unnamable* begins with a similar statement: "What am I to do, what shall I do, what should I do, in my situation, how proceed? By aporia pure and simple? . . . I should mention before going any further, any further on, that I say aporia without knowing what it means. Can one be ephectic otherwise than unawares? I don't know" (291).

Let me uncrumple this much-crumpled thing. In both cases we are exposed to the idea of aporia, and in both cases the speaker hesitates at the word, thereby calling our attention to it. It is only sensible to conclude that aporia is a significant idea. Aporia is skepticism, but skepticism of a particular sort: that skepticism arising from awareness of opposed, unreconcilable views of a subject. In both quotations the speaker denies that he understands the term. The reason for this denial is implied when the Unnamable asks if one can be ephectic—if one can suspend judgment—otherwise than unawares. Obviously if one is deliberately skeptical, if one deliberately suspends judgment as a matter of policy, then one's action is in itself a judgment; pretending to be skeptical, one has actually committed oneself to a belief. Both Beckett and his speakers know better than to fall into that trap.

Aporia, I suggest, explains the structural duality of the novel. Shunted from storyteller to story, from creator to creature, from one world to another, we are kept from settling on either one as the "reality" of the novel, and we can make no resolution of the two. Equally, aporia explains the unsettling vagueness of all the paired terms. To contrive a novel in which a clearly defined creator was opposed to a clearly defined creature and in which other equally specific oppositions were made would be to commit oneself to a belief in duality. True aporia and suspended judgment require that one not be committed even to aporia itself.

What subjects does *Malone Dies* treat aporetically? The old old subjects, truth, reality, identity . . . , all those dead horses flayed throughout Beckett's works. *Malone Dies* is distinguished from his other writings, though, by its attention to the subject of writing itself. Especially since the appearance of Sam and the Addenda in *Watt*, Beckett has intermittently commented on the absurdity of writing (whereas his early monograph *Proust* suggested there was some point to it); and most of his later protagonists have, willy nilly, been their own novelists. But Malone is the only one who approaches the task professionally, taking a postman's holiday at the end of his career, commenting professionally on such topics as the relation between art and life and between author and character, and pointing up the absurdity of it all.

Critical response to Beckett's exploration of this topic has been greatest in France, and the best of the responses is probably Dina Dreyfus' "Vraies et fausses énigmes." [4] She begins by raising the topic at once to a high level: "Beckett's work poses directly the problem proper to the novel and the novelist: what is a novel? What is a novelist? What is the relation of the novelist to the novel? In a word, what are the conditions —not aesthetic but ontological—of the novel?" Her conclusion is devastating to some conventional assumptions about literature:

> The situation of the novelist with regard to his novel is analogous to that of the philosopher and his philosophy, which may be an assertion of the philosopher about Being—a phenomenology—or a revelation of Being to the philosopher—an ontology. Either the novelist tells an invented story, and the story is contingent and relative [i.e., subjective], or the novelist, alienated from his novel, ceases to be its author as that term is rigorously understood. To the extent that this hypothesis appears absurd, one must say that there is and there can be no ontological novel.

That is, no novel—no work of art—can tell us about objective reality or truth. Beckett had reached similar conclusions a decade earlier. In his article "Peintres de l'empêchement" [5] he defined the two kinds

---

[4] *Mercure de France* 331 (October 1957): 268–85.

[5] *Derrière le miroir* (Paris, June 1948), pp. 3–7.

of artist Miss Dreyfus calls ontological and phenomenological: Beckett has one artist complain, "I can't see the object to represent it, because it is what it is"; the other complains, "I can't see the object to represent it, because I am what I am." As Lawrence E. Harvey points out, "Both face the predicament of a sundered world that isolates man irremediably from his surroundings." [6]

So far as *Malone Dies* is concerned with writing, it may be described as a more elaborate exploration of this topic. But it is one thing to say that a literary work contains information and attitudes on a topic, quite another to say that these determine what the work is about or what it means. *Moby Dick* contains much information about whaling, but the novel itself is only trivially about whaling, and its meaning is completely independent of whales. *Malone Dies* contains information about writing, but it does not "mean" about writing. This is not to suggest that its meaning is different from the message Miss Dreyfus has identified. Meaning, for Beckett, is one of those big words which make us so unhappy; it is probable that from his point of view his novels are not meaningfully about anything. The admiring statement he made about Joyce might with equal justice be made about his own work: "His writing is not *about* something; *it is that something itself.*"

Malone Dies is not a *roman à thèse.* It is equally not a psychological novel. I have called attention to the structural use of duality and have related that use to the idea of aporia. It is tempting to conclude that the form of the novel is psychologically imitative, that it imitates the vacillation of the mind between extremes,

> At one extreme agreeing with one Greek,
> At the other agreeing with another Greek,
> Which may be thought, but only so to speak,

and that this vacillation is imposed upon the reader's own mind by means of the novel's structure.

A chief obstacle between that temptation and this conclusion is Beckett's insistence on the chaos of the world. Life is a mess, he believes, and art should not try to reduce it to form. Form belongs to art, not life. Tom Driver quotes Beckett as saying, "The form and the chaos remain separate. The latter is not reduced to the former. That is why the form itself becomes a preoccupation, because it exists as a problem separate from the material it accommodates. To find a form that accommodates

[6] "Samuel Beckett on Life, Art, and Criticism," *Modern Language Notes* 80 (December 1965): 545–62.

the mess, that is the task of the artist now." [7] A year later he told Lawrence Harvey that he knew of no form that did not violate the nature of Being, and said that "if anything new and exciting is going on today, it is the attempt to let Being into art." The relationship between Being and form is unsatisfactory in two respects, it seems. On the one hand, as Beckett pointed out to Harvey, the conventional artistic forms exclude all aspects of Being that don't fit into them; on the other hand, since Being is formless, the impossible best that an artist might achieve would be merely, as he said to Driver, to "find a form that accommodates the mess." Not a form that is or imitates or parallels the form of Being; Being has no form; it can only be accommodated.[8]

About *Malone Dies* one can speak of effects much more surely than of causes or intentions, when one discusses the structure. Its duality has the effect of undermining our assumptions about a straightforward, ascertainable real world; the thing perceived remains obstinately unspecifiable. On the other hand, this duality gives the perceiver no confidence in his perceiving mind. He sees a mess, not a clear and orderly reality, but he cannot see that mess in a clear and orderly way. Both perceiver and perceived are put in question. The same effect occurs when we turn to the topic of truth, or of identity, or indeed to almost any topic raised in the novel; there we are at our old aporetics.

The matter may be stated another way, however. From Beckett's point of view the mess, external and internal, is persistently chaotic. To present it as dualistic, no matter how evasive the dualities, may be to impose artistic form upon it to an unwarrantable degree. Beckett is not given to public evaluations of his work, but his abandonment of such obvious structural elements in his later works[9] may suggest that from his point of view *Malone Dies* is offensively and misleadingly clear.

---

[7] "Beckett by the Madeleine," *Columbia University Forum* 4 (Summer 1961): 21–25.

[8] Cf. Malone's remark, "The forms are many in which the unchanging seeks relief from its formlessness" (197).

[9] Readers of *How It Is*, "Enough," and the late plays may well object here; duality is a consistent element in these works. But it is of one particular kind, I suggest; variations on the theme of the Self and its Voice or the Self and the Other are at the basis of the duality, and not the aporia I have discussed above. This nonaporetic duality is far less important structurally, as *The Unnamable* was the first to suggest.

The Word and Silence in Samuel Beckett's
The Unnamable

by Franco Fanizza

Today many aesthetic systems make the problem of art a question
conditioned by a limited phenomenalism with this or that methodolog-
ical attitude. Isolating aethetics as an autonomous science (particular-
ized in various forms), they tend to distinguish the problem of artistic
value from that of value per se, they tend to reduce the science of art to
a realistic naturalism according to which there's no point in asking
"what is art?" because this would mean "what is life?" and they tend to
reduce the artist to a man who should renounce his being as a man
and characterize himself as a functionary of the "art" business in order
to qualify as an artist. On the other hand, it is not difficult nowadays
to find works that, although from external and only externally limited
points of view aesthetic, embrace the problem of man and of human
behavior in their totality, supported as they are by a tension that one
might call "ontological," without meaning—as severe critics of the philosophical aesthetics do—a return to a sort of meta-aesthetics that the
very presence and urgency of the specific artistic question would dilute
and nullify in the meaningless universe of the traditional philosophic
categories. In this way one realizes that when philosophy asks "what is
art?" it does not aim at discovering the essential value, the ideal model
of artistic expression, but at maintaining those expressions at the level
of effective and authentic human tension, at grasping their inner power
of relation, at going beyond the "sic et nunc" to a point that neither
neo-positivistic aesthetics nor symbolic logic nor the various principles
of verifiability can reach with their limited instruments of analysis, tied
as they are to an obscure and equally old realistic ontology. The en-

"*The Word and Silence in Samuel Beckett's* The Unnamable" *by Franco Fanizza.
From* Aut Aut *60 (November 1960): 380–91. Translated by Barbara Lanotti and J. D.
O'Hara. Reprinted by permission of* Aut Aut.

emy of which art and aesthetics should be wary nowadays is not that
old realism of absolute and normative aesthetics (which have disqual-
ified themselves by now); rather, they ought to beware of the new realism of cultural patterns concealing sociological schemes and ideological interests that reduce the problematical impact of the artistic
language by discriminating between what is verifiable and what is emo-
tional. These yardsticks of criticism prevent the comprehension of new
languages, languages that, according to their function, by turns dialec-
tically destructive and constructive, are either silence or authentic word.

Moreover one should add that as soon as those cultural patterns are
transformed, as inevitably happens, into absolute values, they tend to
diseducate art itself, which then becomes the producer of objects demanded by the sociological market or by the ideology of the establish-
ment. When the artist lowers himself to the commonplace, when he
adopts the stance of cultural realism, then the specific aesthetic inten-
tionality of his work really subordinates itself to the current taste, to
the public demand: the artist turns into the hidden persuader. Since at
that stage the work lacks the problematical tension that makes art the
difficult and often desperate attempt at a relation not ontologically
guaranteed, the artistic object becomes an artistic "product." After this
transformation, what is left is no longer art as an autonomous attitude,
but art as a system of external relations. If it does not become the instrument of ideological deceit or purely economic value, art becomes
play or a luxurious accessory of the soul, one of several expedients to
make the sleep of the soul more pleasant. While within this dimension
art can show itself apparently engaged with reality, in truth it is only,
in this case, the re-exposition of a "this-and-this" reality, found and
constated as such, without allowing the slightest importance to the
problem of being of this reality.

Of the renunciation of schemes and cultural patterns and, consequently, of the impossibility of separating the problem of man from
the problem of the artist, we find significant examples in the works of
Samuel Beckett. It would be difficult to attempt an examination of
B.'s work according to contemporary aesthetic principles, namely,
evincing its meaning, or rather giving it a meaning. Precisely because
in B. there is a different ontological dimension, there is a new aesthetic
dimension, or better, there is the problem of the foundation of an
aesthetic. Therefore all attempts to "find" a meaning in his work have
failed, because his word is an accusation against culture rather than a
cultural datum; rather than taking pleasure in expression, it puts the

problem of expression at the crossroads of word and silence. Hence the complexity and at the same time the "futility" of B.'s works. It is not easy to understand B. because his works request from the reader this same change of basis, of the very foundation of this basis. No writer ever demanded from his reader or audience a deeper collaboration, consisting mainly in spiritual tension and in a continuous stimulus toward the pure question. This stimulus, which is the renunciation of the concluding word, is the only feature common to all B.'s works, B. being extremely diffident towards others and not less so towards himself. This distrust leads him always to adopt a different problematic intonation in each of his works, which are, each in its own terms, a problematically complete world, though liable always to fundamental changes. It is therefore difficult to find exact correspondences between his dramatic works and his *récits* or even among the latter alone. He changes his discourse according to a problematic perspective that cannot be anticipated because it is not systematic, and because the language functions in close relation to the heart. B. does not introduce himself as the artist-bard or as the chronicler of the soul, but as man, or rather as men (disintegrated psychologically and spiritually) in the middle of the falls and contradictions of a labored and ambivalent process of growth. Before life, in its chaotic futility and ambiguity, full of nonsense, in its illusory but inviting certainty, B. presents himself with a vital adherence that does not allow him to linger long in one place but obliges him to move continuously. He is always in an aesthetic state like that of the Kirkegaardian seducer who would be able to use a magic wand in the most banal way—like cleaning his pipe with it. At every step he wins back and loses everything, at every step he starts over again, thus making his meaningless word highly significant without any of those absolutist pretensions often implied in the artistic process whenever the artistic language, instead of keeping the problem open and increasing its impact, presumes to conclude it forever. However, if on the one hand this conclusiveness makes the process of comprehension less tiring for the reader and for the critic, on the other hand it is also the most evident sign of the exhaustion of the artist. The strength of B.'s works, on the contrary, lies in their continuous, renewed, and always renewing youth. Therefore one can realize how fresh and up to date his works are—except for him who, distracted by a too restricted image of his time, is deaf to those voices that, because of their originality and their different and new wave length, speak to everybody and to nobody. Because of this, if on the one hand B.'s works are an accusation against

our culture and a protest against it, on the other hand they are also a
very lively image of the reality in which we are living and also evidence
that it is still possible to achieve vitality, even if, in order to do so, we
have to refer to chaos or to an apparent absurd. On a literary level
they are demonstrations of the infinite possibilities of artistic language
—something very similar to the dodecaphonic musical language.

Because of the above-mentioned unsystematicity in B.'s works, it is
difficult or impossible for the critic to grasp the true appearance (if
Beckett has one) of their universe. Given, therefore, the lack of even
the slightest common denominator among his various artistic stages,[1]
one can only address oneself in good faith—already an attempt at a
critical interpretation—to whichever one holds to be his most valid attitude before the enigma. And since there is not, rigorously, a beginning
or an end in B.'s works, it seems to us that one can find his most significant word in the novel-*récit The Unnamable*. In this work, we say,
is contained his final (not in a chronological sense) "word." Therefore,
and without claiming to exhaust the meaning of B.'s works in this essay, we will analyze that novel.

The definitive traditional modes with which to approach a reality
that is always both discovered and presupposed—the categories, that is,
of space, relation, time, and substance—are by now useless. They prove
themselves inconsistent in B.'s works. This is not because of their inef-
fectiveness (we are not questioning here their nullity or their reality),
but mainly because there has been a total suspension of the "me" and
"outside me," a loss of the sense of the "I" and "not-I." This newly in-
stituted "no-nothingness" (because by saying "nothingness" one would
indirectly admit the existence of a nullifying principle, and then the
word would have a meaning, since nothingness would still be a theme
able to maintain an internally coherent monologue as in Sartre's
Nausea[2]), in short, this sudden, immediate, apparently unjustified re-
ascent to the chaos of the non-determinate, of the non-thinking ("think
no more about anything, think no more" [336]), this return to the eter-

---

[1] I cannot believe that Beckett's theatrical personages are the personalization and
objectification of the "uncertain shadows" "barely glimpsed in the novels." Cf. C.
Fruttero, "Introduction" to the Italian translation of *Waiting for Godot* (Turin,
1956), p. 14.

[2] Cf. P. de Boisdeffre, *Une histoire vivante de la littérature d'aujourd'hui* (Paris,
1959), p. 303: 'We are far from the beautiful organized monologues of *Nausea*, which
develops the same theme, but in which the resources of an accomplished rhetoric are
found placed in the service of that which denies it."

nal as to something that, lacking an end, lacks even a beginning—all this leads us to the impossibility of questioning, to the negation of the human *type,* if—as Aristotle holds—the characteristic of man rests in his positive thaumazein and his self-determination and self-qualification in the objectivity furnished by the senses. According to Hegel, the ego in man "is also the transition from undifferentiated indeterminacy to the *differentiation, determination,* and *positing* of a determinacy as a content and object. Now further, this content may either be given by nature or engendered by the concept of mind. Through this positing of itself as something *determinate, the ego steps* in principle *into determinate existence.* This is the absolute moment, the *finitude* or *particularization* of the ego." [3] Here, on the contrary, "there is no more logical discourse, eloquence, or irony: we are beyond all that, lost in the visceral consciousness, almost microscopic, of an intelligent corpuscle, of a soul on the point of being expelled from its fleshly envelope, and whose consciousness turns toward the void, beyond all control of the intelligence or the reason, freed already from the world, but not from this agonizing Me that it still endures, with which it is going to die." [4] "Where now? Who now? When now? Unquestioning. I, say I. Unbelieving. Questions, hypotheses, call them that. Keep going, going on, call that going, call that on." "It, say it, not knowing what." "I seem to speak, it is not I, about me, it is not about me." "What am I to do, what shall I do, what should I do, in my situation, how proceed?" (291) This literal lack of beginning, this condition of non-birth or, better, of pre-birth is B.'s world. It is the content of his human existence and the material of his poetic universe. Without intending it systematically, Beckett has achieved the phenomenological *epoché,* although without finding the transcendental ego. He has achieved the anti-novel, the anti-literature based on the anti-human. He has linked *Angst* with nausea and has gone beyond them; all this, because from the beginning he has set himself outside any socio-cultural-worldly structure, avoiding the world as a source of value or meaning, as a biological, situational, existential matrix. He has isolated himself in his disorderly spiritual autobiography, and that analysis has gradually dissolved any participation or principle of participation. He is not available for the "this-is-this" world. "The thing to avoid, I don't know why, is the spirit of system. People with

---

[3] Hegel, *The Philosophy of Right,* trans. T. M. Knox, Introduction, paragraph 6. Italics added.

[4] Boisdeffre, pp. 303f.

things, people without things, things without people, what does it
matter, I flatter myself it will not take me long to scatter them, whenever I choose, to the winds. I don't see how. The best would be not to
begin. But I have to begin. That is to say I have to go on" (292). Nor
do his artistic antecedents in earlier works constitute a unifying process.
Malone and Molloy, who seem to pursue him with their world and
their problems, are soon abandoned to their fate. Nevertheless, despite
everything, cries B., "I am here" (301), and "I shall never be silent.
Never" (291). "The search for the means to put an end to things, an
end to speech, is what enables the discourse to continue" (299). To
continue, but where, and for how long?

> Unfortunately I am afraid, as always, of going on. For to go on means
> going from here, means finding me, losing me, vanishing and beginning
> again, a stranger first, then little by little the same as always, in another
> place, where I shall say I have always been, of which I shall know noth-
> ing, being incapable of seeing, moving, thinking, speaking, but of which
> little by little, in spite of these handicaps, I shall begin to know some-
> thing, just enough for it to turn out to be the same place as always, the
> same which seems made for me and does not want me, which I seem to
> want and do not want, take your choice, which spews me out or swallows
> me up, I'll never know, which is perhaps merely the inside of my distant
> skull where once I wandered, now am fixed, lost for tininess, or straining
> against the walls, with my head, my hands, my feet, my back, and ever
> murmuring my old stories, my old story, as if it were the first time. (302f.)

To move, to speak, but to say what? The voice, says B., "is not mine,
I have none, I have no voice and must speak, that is all I know, it's
round that I must revolve, of that I must speak, with this voice that
is not mine, but can only be mine, since there is no one but me, or
if there are others, to whom it might belong, they have never come
near me . . ." (307).

"If I could speak and yet say nothing, really nothing?" (303) And
at this point it is not clear whether Beckett is unable to talk or has
nothing to say; probably the two are indissolubly linked. Often to speak
does not mean anything but to utter words with which we are not
concerned. "For it is difficult to speak, even any old rubbish, and at
the same time focus one's attention on another point, where one's
true interest lies, as fitfully defined by a feeble murmur seeming to
apologize for not being dead" (308). Similarly, "it is all very fine to
keep silence, but one has also to consider the kind of silence one keeps"

(309). Not the inauthentic silence, but the authentic one of protest, of non-participation, of absolute non-engagement. However, let us beware; it is not the case of a choice but of having been chosen. The drama and at the same time the destiny of Samuel Beckett is that of "having to speak." "I have to speak, whatever that means. Having nothing to say, no words but the words of others, I have to speak. No one compels me to, there is no one, it's an accident, a fact" (314). "I was given a pensum, at birth perhaps, as a punishment for having been born perhaps, or for no particular reason, because they dislike me, and I've forgotten what it is" (310). Therefore, despite everything, there remains an *I* that is simply *word,* an *I-thinking-word. Word* in Beckett, while avoiding all facile consonance with other words, while seeking to achieve eloquent silence, still wills to live. There is a fundamental contradiction in his use of language: in order to destroy itself and rise to the authentic silence, the word must be voice, an uttered expression, a thing said, in protest against the subjugation and slavery of the commonplace, of habit, of conformity to so-called values. To re-achieve the word, B. has to speak even if to deny or to execrate.

> There is no use denying, no use harping on the same old thing I know so well, and so easy to say, and which simply amounts in the end to speaking yet again in the way they intend me to speak, that is to say about them, even with execration and disbelief. . . . There's no getting rid of them without naming them and their contraptions, that's the thing to keep in mind. (326)

But despite all the burden of this contradiction, despite the fact that at every step he realizes his dependence upon a world and a language not his own, which soil him with their burdensome heritage of prejudices, and despite the fact that his path is not a straight line but a continuous spiral of lapses and relapses into the identical mistakes, Samuel Beckett aspires to "die under his own steam," to do without the *données* of those continually presupposed and continually discovered human structures, to find himself outside of the current cultural humanism. "If I ever succeed in dying under my own steam, then they will be in a better position to decide if I am worthy to adorn another age, or to try the same one again, with the benefit of my experience" (330). In order to find oneself, one has to situate oneself outside the game, outside the world. It is not easy to say where this will lead, whether to a new world or to the destruction of the old and nothing more. To escape the world's culture or to be abandoned by it is for Beckett to be restored at last to oneself.

But at the moment when Beckett re-achieves everything, at the same moment he loses everything, and all begins again. His evasions, for this reason, have no system, even if they are indeterminately programmed. "And my course is not helicoidal, I got that wrong too, but a succession of irregular loops, now sharp and short as in the waltz, now of a parabolic sweep that embraces entire boglands, now between the two, somewhere or other, and invariably unpredictable in direction, that is to say determined by the panic of the moment" (327). The *I-thinking-word* is not a transcendental principle capable of directing an ascesis, of fixing itself in a character.

> At no moment do I know what I'm talking about, nor of whom, nor of where, nor how, nor why, but I could employ fifty wretches for this sinister operation and still be short of a fifty-first, to close the circuit, that I know, without knowing what it means. The essential is never to arrive anywhere, never to be anywhere, neither where Mahood is, nor where Worm is, nor where I am, it little matters thanks to what dispensation. The essential is to go on squirming forever at the end of the line, as long as there are waters and banks and ravening in heaven a sporting God to plague his creature, per pro his chosen shits. (338)

Life for Beckett is *Erlebnis*, a continuous flowing, in which he appears and disappears in a punctualized, continuing, fragmentary, and hopeless fight against this flow. Or, as he seems to say, in a chaotic and caustic symbolism, human existence is an enforced habitation in a jar. The being there enclosed, which can barely be recognized as a man, is aided or, better, closely watched by a woman (Nature?) who uses him for her own obscure ends. The being of this prisoner is lacerated by confusion, humiliation, and pain. On the other hand, he no longer hopes to change his condition, even if he were brought to another place and left completely to himself, after being mutilated, swollen, unrecognizable, stripped of any distinctive quality. In this strange analysis by Beckett there is a sense of uneasiness, of nausea, of depression and decay that mingles flesh and spirit; and from it all emanates a stink of monstrous, horripilant, disgusting and rotten carnality. But once abandoned to himself, says B., "it's a lot to expect of one creature, it's a lot to ask, that he should first behave as if he were not, then as if he were, before being admitted to that peace where he neither is, nor is not, and where the language dies that permits of such expressions. Two falsehoods, two trappings, to be borne to the end, before I can be let loose, alone, in the unthinkable unspeakable, where I have not ceased to be, where they will not let me be" (334f.). An analysis that is the convulsive discovery of a state of annihilation and isolation, of complete alienation recognizing itself as such. "Here many ages of accusation against the world reach an end: man's humiliation, which, from Rousseau to Kafka, paralyzes so many writers, culminates here in a world of abjection and ignominy. Beings judge themselves 'in the tranquillity of decomposition' (25), reviewing their life as if they were already damned, and mingling forever with their solitude, their humiliation, and their unhappiness before disappearing in an ocean of ordure." [5]

And in this condition, Beckett turns to say, "It's a question of voices, of voices to keep going, in the right manner, when they stop, on purpose, to put me to the test, as now the one whose burden is roughly to the effect that I am alive. Warmth, ease, conviction, the right manner, as if it were my own voice, pronouncing my own words, words pronouncing me alive, since that's how they want me to be, I don't know why, with their billions of quick, their trillions of dead, that's not enough for them, I too must contribute my little convulsion, mewl, howl, gasp and rattle, loving my neighbour and blessed with reason" (335). But the word, like all that my soul says to itself, is something alien that doesn't belong to me. "It is they who dictate this torrent of balls, they who stuffed me full of these groans that choke me" (335): words of certainty, fruits of the blessing of reason, but with a more important impact than in Pascal. Samuel Beckett affirms that "I have to puke my heart out too, spew it up whole along with the rest of the vomit, it's then at last I'll look as if I mean what I'm saying, it won't be just idle words" (335f.). Just now, however, we have nothing but words that we must speak, "orders, prayers, threats, praise, reproach, reasons" (337). Just a little longer, says B., and "I'll fall down dead, worn out by the rudiments" (337).

But, at the end, what does Samuel Beckett want, who is he? "I am he who will never be caught, never delivered, who crawls between the thwarts, towards the new day that promises to be glorious, festooned with lifebelts, praying for rack and ruin" (339). Who is Beckett? A wavering between word and silence, between forced participation and renunciation. "It's not I speaking, it's not I hearing, let us not

---

[5] Boisdeffre, p. 304.

go into that, let us go on as if I were the only one in the world, whereas I'm the only one absent from it, or with others, what difference does it make, others present, others absent, they are not obliged to make themselves manifest, all that is needed is to wander and let wander, be this slow boundless whirlwind and every particle of its dust, it's impossible. Someone speaks, someone hears, no need to go any further . . ." (401). And then . . . "the silence, speak of the silence before going into it, was I there already, I don't know, at every instant I'm there, listen to me speaking of it, I knew it would come, I emerge from it to speak of it, I stay in it to speak of it, if it's I who speak, and it's not, I act as if it were, sometimes I act as if it were, but at length, was I ever there at length, a long stay, I understand nothing about duration, I can't speak of it, oh I know I speak of it, I say never and ever, I speak of the four seasons and the different parts of the day and night, the night has no parts, that's because you are asleep, the seasons must be very similar, perhaps it's springtime now, that's all words they taught me, without making their meaning clear to me, that's how I learnt to reason, I use them all, all the words they showed me . . ." (407). "It will be the silence, for a moment, a good few moments, or it will be mine, the lasting one, that didn't last, that still lasts, it will be I, you must go on, I can't go on, you must go on, I'll go on, you must say words, as long as there are any, until they find me, until they say me, strange pain, strange sin, you must go on, perhaps it's done already, perhaps they have said me already, perhaps they have carried me to the threshold of my story, before the door that opens on my story, that would surprise me, if it opens, it will be I, it will be the silence, where I am. I don't know, I'll never know, in the silence you don't know, you must go on, I can't go on, I'll go on" (414).

To go on, not in the spirit of one returning to the fold, but like the young Crusoe, after the first unfortunate attempt to escape from his native York towards the open sea, despite all the sad posthumous afflictions of shipwreck, trying again and always trying again.

Words that tend to shape and verify themselves in the silence: this datum is the most significant, though provisory and problematic, in Beckett's work. This "howling" silence, however, is one of the most passionate, powerful, and caustic protests against contemporary humanism. Its strength lies in the virginity of its howl, in the delirious raving of his word, in the irritable renunciation of any mundane-humane participation. The latter, however one realizes it or even attempts to realize it, represents the debasing of any honest gesture, as though one soiled oneself in the forms of unmoving conformity, letting oneself decay into mechanical animality and presumptuous stupidity. And finally, losing the "meaning" and the "value" of the true silence, letting oneself be dominated by the voices of a world of anonymous indifference and radical moral filthiness, a world in which, despite reason's protests, the dignity of intelligence is lost. Against such a world the howl of Samuel Beckett has a regenerative force beyond any pleasure in expression, beyond any aesthetic arrogance. The Beckettian protest, as has often been pointed out, is also against culture, culture being a hybrid scheme, a reality falsely postulated as valid, a produced and manipulated reality. Anti-culture is a return, by way of falls and errors, to a wider perspective, infinitely vaster, in which language, and with it contemporary man, through a regenerating fall into silence and chaos, finally achieve a meaning.

Style in the Trilogy

by Ludovic Janvier

Two Writers at Work

The language-space in which *Molloy* is written will appear less worked over in its details than that of the *Nouvelles*, undoubtedly aiming at a quite different total impression. A story immense and rich in situations, this great edifice of writing treats writing in a more casual manner, and introduces into the perfection of a style like that of "The Expelled" the notion of risk, of improvisation, of gambling: it adds *hesitation* to its speech.

This point in the development of Beckett's style having been reached, it is necessary to specify that this new dimension undergoes various treatments here. *Molloy* is divided into two contrapuntal periods, as we know, and while the long phrase and the unforced tone characterize Molloy's adventures, those of Moran are narrated mainly in a brief and dogmatic style that best conveys his pretentious efforts at moral rigor and his puritanic arrogance. On this level, the two styles are opposed. But Moran's language crumbles, and it is in this collapse, which causes the sentences of incisive hardness to evolve toward a stumbling softness almost like Molloy's, that we best can read the lamentable and humorous collapse by which, as we have seen, Moran is forced to move closer to the character of Molloy. On this level, there is only one style.

Before he reached that stage, what characterized Moran's style was a rhythm broken not only on the page by more frequent paragraphing, but within the paragraphs by occasional brief sentences, and within the sentences by elementary syntactical groups, the whole capable of giving the impression of an ossification of language. This is what constitutes that celebrated beginning, that "spiteful" and decisive

"Style in the Trilogy" (Editor's title). From Pour Samuel Beckett by Ludovic Janvier (Paris: Les Éditions de Minuit, 1966), pp. 231–41. Translated by J. D. O'Hara. Reprinted by permission of the publisher.

attack, whose rigor imposes itself on the memory thanks to the sands in which Molloy, on the preceding pages, had bogged down. Such a language is maintained at times by an aggressive use of consonants, notably in the lively dialogues between Moran and his servant, his son, and the parish priest—an oral aggression of which one can hear echoes even in the choice of his name, Moran, in opposition to the diluted vocable Molloy; and in the recurrence of names like Martha and Gaber; in the importance of such verbs as *to cry, to exclaim, to shout* within the conversations and the narrative. We might add an occasional haste in the composition matching the protagonist's fits of temper, and we have all the elements contributing to the irritable tone of the first pages of Moran's narrative and, because of their vigor, placing those pages among the writer's best achievements. Quivering all over with the impatience of his speech, Moran is heard growing excited and tearing his hair as, with his son, he prepares to depart:

> Next I attacked, according to my custom, the capital question of the effects to take with me. And on this subject too I should have come to a quite otiose decision, but for my son, who burst in wanting to know if he might go out. I controlled myself. He was wiping his mouth with the back of his hand, a thing I do not like to see. But there are nastier gestures. I speak from experience.
> Out? I said. Where? Out! Vagueness I abhor. I was beginning to feel hungry. To the Elms, he replied. So we call our little public park. And yet there is not an elm to be seen in it, I have been told. What for? I said. To go over my botany, he replied. There were times I suspected my son of deceit. This was one. I would almost have preferred him to say, For a walk, or, To look at the tarts. The trouble was he knew far more than I, about botany. Otherwise I could have set him a few teasers, on his return. Personally I just liked plants in all innocence and simplicity. I even saw in them at times a superfetatory proof of the existence of God. Go, I said, but be back at half-past four. I want to talk to you. Yes papa, he said. Yes papa! Ah! (99)

The ample discursive flow of Molloy's narrative and of Moran's when he reaches that level is filled with all the marvels of improvisation, as we have said, and imitates the progress of speech. Such a principle of indecision, by its entry even into the workings of the book, deserves recognition for its profound originality: the writing itself is its own subject, and Molloy and Moran are two writers at work.

There is, for instance, the dilution of a topic in details that are

born from it and that keep the narrative going. There is the repetition
of a term as an echo, as if the writer had left it until he could recast
the sentence, the paragraph, the book. The two phenomena may be
combined: "So I put on my clothes, having first made sure they had
not been tampered with, that is to say I put on my trousers, my greatcoat, my hat and my boots. My boots. They came up to where . . ."
(46).

This propping of words by words is revealed by the use of that
sentence crutch that forms the sentence's beginning by restating the
previous sentence's object, repeated then by a pronoun (". . . and my
boots. My boots. They . . ."). In barely two pages there are three
examples: "The house where Lousse lived. Must I describe it? . . .
My life, my life, now I speak of it as something over. . . . But these
cullions, I must be attached to them after all . . ." (35f.). Here this
inversion is not merely a means of setting in relief, or even the result
of an attempt at varying the construction: rather it is a matter of
recasting the conventional phrasing; and the resulting insistence is
one of those means that serve to push the discourse forward, relying
on a forceful oral phrasing and making us stick to its rhythm. Beckett
here compares with another great "oral" writer, Céline, in whose
style the propulsive role played by that positioning of the sentence's
object is extremely important. Reading him, too, one listens, reflects,
and imitates.

Oral style: it is the liberty of speech, in fact, that introduces
here—to a different degree than in Céline, of course—all the means
of flexibility in the long unparagraphed narrative managed so well
by Molloy, and permits the unconstrained narrator to give us this:
"For if you set out to mention everything you would never be done,
and that's what counts, to be done, to have done. Oh I know, even
when you mention only a few of the things there are, you do not get
done either, I know, I know" (41), and this: "I had stolen from
Lousse a little silver, oh nothing much, massive teaspoons" (63), and
the hesitant itemization that ends: "What else, ah yes, carobs, so dear
to goats" (85).

Exclamations and interrogations interrupt the narrator with abrupt
brakings, the halt accentuated by the speed of the sentence: then the
machine starts up again without coming apart farther, sometimes
aided at the most unexpected moments by whimsical conjugations:
since, but, therefore, playing at once the role of a casual link appro-

priate to assure the continuity of the process and that of a link too strong not to betray its proper usage as a logical connective. "It was from this cloud," Molloy suggests clumsily to us, "the above rain was falling." And he adds, heaping logic on itself, what will make the passage explode in admirable humor: "See how things hang together. And as to making up my mind which quarter of the heaven was the least gloomy, it was no easy matter. For at first sight the heavens seemed uniformly gloomy. But by taking a little pains, for there were moments in my life when I took a little pains, I obtained a result, that is to say I came to a decision in the matter. So I was able to continue on my way, saying, I am going towards the sun, that is to say in theory towards the East" (62).

Logic and illogic by turns: elsewhere, the humor of Beckett's quiet virtuosity uses as weapons parodies of particular jargons. In the philosophic style, there is the well-known series of "questions of a theological nature" posed by the imperturbable Moran; there is the false dilemma of the open umbrella, the words changing places in a brief panic (171); and there is the delightful, barely perceptible parody of overly pretty language to which Moran abruptly yields, the sentiment of proprietorship growing as languid as a dream: "And birds of course, blackbird and thrush, their song sadly dying, vanquished by the heat, and leaving dawn's high boughs for the bushes' gloom. Contentedly I inhaled the scent of my lemon-verbena" (93).

All these features, finally, report the one important occurrence that justifies them all, from the hesitant speech[1] and the oral exclamation to the expressive recasting, including them in the enormous unbroken flow that carries them and uses them: that occurrence— two writers are at grips with words. Molloy writes from his mother's room in the conditions we know. Under the lamp, Moran draws up his report. They seek words to tell their story, and the adventure that they have been living ever since no longer concerns them; their concern is with language. Their adventure no longer concerns the past of beings, but the future of words. They are in danger. This march toward the heart, undertaken under constraint, is nevertheless the undeniable expression of a freedom; and what makes so close to us the jeopardy of these men totally engaged in gambling on

---

[1] On p. 45 two remarkable examples are grouped together. One of them: "And then doing fills me with such a, I don't know, impossible to express, for me, now . . ." and the sentence remains suspended on that unnamable.

language's leading to the very end, is precisely their presence, almost their breathing as they do it.

More and better than a tragedy, more than an exercise in humor, that is *Molloy*: the human presence of the writer at work within his work—that is to say, the effort of man to speak.

Departure of Words, Words of Departure

That gamble will never cease to be accentuated, moreover, answering to the need, in proportion to the work's progress, to search by means of words and to speak that search. But while the supple sentences of *Molloy* made us sense a certain distance between ourselves and the narrator despite his engagement in the enterprise and his hesitations of speech, the diction of *Malone Dies* and *The Unnamable* is filled with all the signs of a more dramatic experience. We cannot yet speak of a general crushing of discourse such as we will experience in the exceptional *How It Is*; nevertheless, we must consider the two great works that precede it as the place for a kind of mutation of speech or pulverizing of superfluous syntactic elements in which the reduction of the sentence's essential segments and the weakening of the rhythm play the most active part.

Up to this point the sentence could be bewildered, as it were, by the introduction of oral processes. We see it there finally broken because the thought is no longer enclosed within the limits, no matter how simple, of a sequence or of half-sequences; rather, it is diluted through many of them, and even approaches contradiction in order more successfully to imitate the regrets and reversals of the first formulation: "I shall therefore die of old age pure and simple," the character Malone thinks and writes, "glutted with days as in the days before the flood, on a full stomach." A possibility. But this possibility is then denied, and the contradiction opens itself to other echoing contradictions: "Perhaps they think I am dead. Or perhaps they are dead themselves. I say they, though perhaps I should not" (252f.).

The idea is developed and denied to the rough rhythm of several sentences. Elsewhere there are one-word sentences, answering to some elementary need. When one knows that at the same time the character himself is undergoing the same treatment within that speech so increasingly rigorous with itself and unkind to its subjects, then the language appears to a remarkable degree the revelator of being.

This unloading of the sentence, enervating the progress of the narrative and propelling it by fits and starts, will express itself as what one might call style with engine trouble. The grammatical coordination in *Molloy* is noticeably erased, advantageously setting off the contents of the syntactic units; but the sentence itself can be pulverized to the advantage of the verb or the noun, notably at the beginning of a paragraph; and this triggers a long series, because on this brutal affirmation-restart depends the difficult continuance of the enterprise.

Emphasis on the verb: "Live and invent. I have tried. I must have tried. Invent" (194), and the impulse given by the infinitive puts the discourse again into gear. "We are getting on" (193), Malone says elsewhere, and it is half a statement, half encouragement to go on.

Special emphasis on the noun. One even doubts that the verb can be without contradiction the sole propulsive element, or even the principal one. After a hole, a blank, even in the middle of the narrative when it has broken down or simply reached a dead end through inadvertence and fatigue, it is the noun's direct echo, reminder, or statement of what came before, that facilitates the narrative's resumption—not the verb's command, demanding action too abruptly from writing suspended precisely in default of activity. In this respect the first thirty pages of *Malone Dies* are revelatory; there are so many restarts accomplished through these maieutic formulas: "Present state. This room seems to be mine. . . . What tedium. . . . The summer holidays. In the morning he took private lessons. . . . The market. The inadequacy of the exchanges. . . . The peasants. His visits to. . . . The Lamberts. The Lamberts found it difficult to live. . . . The farm. The farm was in a hollow. . . . Dead world, airless, waterless. That's it, reminisce" (182, 187, 189, 194, 196, 199, 201).

Once the impetus has been given, the speech winds on. But when Malone, exhausted and near that death we never will know, no longer has the strength to speak, the rhythm will suddenly recreate itself, and it is these same gasps of encouragement that—after a blank space and a silence—will bring the narrative back to life. A verb: "I feel. I feel it's coming" (233). Nouns: "Quick, quick my possessions" (246). "A thousand little things to report" (259). "Inauspicious beginnings indeed" (263). "Moll. I'm going to kill her" (264). "A last effort" (266). "The wagonette" (284). "The boat. Room, as in the wagonette . . ." (285). "The island. A last effort. The islet" (286).

This use of nouns, which we have called maieutic and of which *Malone Dies* and *The Unnamable* offer many examples, illustrates

best, perhaps, the painful emergence of words. To that quality of risk
discussed above there is now added the essential value that makes this
enterprise closer to us than any other. The voice speaks frankly; we
hear it gasp for breath; its false starts and erasures persuade us completely of our kinship with it. "Dead world, airless, waterless. That's
it, reminisce. Here and there, in the bed of a crater, the shadow of
a withered lichen. And nights of three hundred hours. Dearest of
lights, wan, pitted, least fatuous of lights. That's it, babble" (201).

Questions, asides, exclamations, single words, interruptions, and
blanks marking air-pockets—often dramatic ones—all signifying here
a speech that is always uttered, devised, with uncertain prospects.
Malone speaks, but he dies. And while this dying is certainly
a physical ruin, it is also the precarious life, the inevitable destruction
of words born fragilely one from the other and risking their future
in proportion as they urge each other forward.

Seeking itself and repeatedly breaking down, this style of writing
brings to the page the first examples of "quaqua" speech—if I may
describe the phenomenon with a word borrowed from *How It Is* and
from Lucky's monologue in *Waiting for Godot*. In the middle of a
torrent of words disconnected from their meaning, Lucky stumbles on
certain formulas and repeats them, disjoints them, sinks into them,
and varies his crazed discourse with spectacular failures, his repeated
"quaqua . . . quaquaquaqua" marking so many moments when
language, uncontrolled, slips out from under itself. Extreme weariness,
lack of breath, or loss of sense because of automation of the power
of speech and stupefaction of thought—the collapse of Lucky and of
How It Is will be understood more clearly if we connect it to its
source, which is here; specifically, this almost echolalic tendency can be
seen here, articulated as it is by the insularity of the words and the
suffering of the man who ventures to speak them. This page of *Malone
Dies* says scarcely anything else:

> Weary with my weariness, white last moon, sole regret, not even. To be
> dead, before her, on her, with her, and turn, dead on dead, about poor
> mankind, and never have to die any more, from among the living. Not
> even, not even that. My moon was here below, far below, the little I was
> able to desire. And one day, soon, soon, one earthlit night, beneath the
> earth, a dying being will say, like me, in the earthlight, Not even, not
> even that, and die, without having been able to find a regret. (264)

Here and now this cruel game of repetitions should be put in relation to the sado-masochism peculiar to the Beckett character. Words referring only to themselves, turning in the language-space as if caged, ill and the repetition of ill: we are face to face with that well-known page of *The Unnamable* that it is impossible not to quote again, since there the suffering of being born by means of words, in knowing mortal speech, of going out of one's self toward oneself, a step continually to be repeated, this suffering is no longer tolerable; at the end of the words there are always the words that make us undiscoverable, and these words then run mad:

> Wherever I go I find me, leave me, go towards me, come from me, nothing ever but me, a particle of me, retrieved, lost, gone astray, I'm all these words, these strangers, this dust of words, with no ground for their settling, no sky for their dispersing, coming together to say, fleeing one another to say, that I am they, all of them, those that merge, those that part, those that never meet, and nothing else, yes, something else, that I'm something quite different, a quite different thing, a wordless thing in an empty place, a hard shut dry cold black place, where nothing stirs, nothing speaks, and that I listen, and that I seek, like a caged beast born of caged beasts born of caged beasts born of caged beasts born in a cage and dead in a cage, born and then dead, born in a cage and then dead in a cage. . . . (386f.)

The contradictoriness of language and its major stumbling to speak the self that seeks itself through it, these are rendered in an oral substance whose richness raises *Malone Dies* and especially *The Unnamable* perhaps to the summit of discursive achievement in Beckett's work.

Because this last work, besides the passages in which its main drift is magisterially sketched, bears astonishingly forceful phrases. Their density, bordering on that of a Rimbaud, a Pascal, an Artaud, draws its power from the short-circuit it induces between tenderness and violence.

"Currish obscurity, to thy kennel, hell-hound!" (362)

"A big stone, and faithful, that would be better than nothing, pending the hearts of flesh" (363).

"Strange task, which consists in speaking of oneself. Strange hope, turned towards silence and peace" (311).

"Let us go on as if I were the only one in the world, whereas I'm the only one absent from it" (401).

"Today is the first day, it begins, I know it well, I'll remember it as I go along, all adown it I'll be born and born, births for nothing, and come to night without having been. Look at this Tunis pink, it's dawn" (400).

And finally this admirable sentence:

"Lashed to the stake, blindfold, gagged to the gullet, you take the air, under the elms in se, murmuring Shelley, impervious to the shafts" (393).

In these accomplishments all Beckett's qualities are condensed to add to that endless murmur in our ear the force, the pungency that tip his mortal enterprise toward the living eternity of perfection.

God and Samuel Beckett

by Richard N. Coe

The universe of Samuel Beckett is certainly as complex as that of any other living writer. Yet it is not a dream-universe, like that of Jarry or Ionesco. It is a metaphysical vision of ultimate "reality," constructed out of innumerable threads of logic tightly interwoven, out of fragmented arguments from Proust and Descartes, from Geulincx, Malebranche and Schopenhauer, from Dostoievsky, Wittgenstein and Sartre, each seemingly irrefutable, each in its right and proper place, and each rushing headlong towards an inescapable impossibility. It is a universe precariously balanced between opposing forces— between positive and negative—and whenever we examine the structure too attentively, positive and negative quietly cancel each other out and leave a Void: a Nothingness which is somehow more real than the once solid-seeming structure of impossibilities whose place it has taken. Bit by bit, as Murphy comes to realize, "the somethings give way, or perhaps simply add up, to the Nothing, than which in the guffaw of the Abderite naught is more real." [1]

Like their creator, Beckett's "people," one and all, are uncompromising rationalists. Incessantly they ask themselves questions. "Where now? Who now? When now?" queries The Unnamable—only to discover that, in so far as there is any credible "reality," it lies, not in the answer, but in the question. For in effect the questions which Beckett's people ask, however reasonably, are precisely those which reason cannot answer. Left to its own devices (and yet it has no other resource), their reason cannot tell them with certainty a single thing that they want to know; not so much as whether (perhaps) they are already dead, or (maybe) still alive. "That may come in useful,"

"God and Samuel Beckett" by Richard N. Coe. From Meanjin Quarterly *(March 1965): 66–85. Reprinted by permission of* Meanjin Quarterly.
[1] *Murphy.* N.Y. (Grove Press), n.d. [1958?], p. 246.

remarks Molloy (14), optimistically, concerning the latter hypothesis—but a hypothesis it remains for all that. Their ultimate identity is an enigma, their existence at any given moment an improbability. "So there you are again," asserts Vladimir; and Estragon, with that refined concern for truth which characterises all Beckett's people, counters simply "Am I?" [2] They are all strangers and sojourners in the current dimensions of existence; like the narrator of Proust's *A la Recherche du Temps Perdu*—in whom most of them have their remoter origins—they know themselves exiled from their true domain of being, alienated from their proper "selves," imprisoned against their will in space and more particularly in time. Yet their attempts to escape from these arbitrary absolutes are futile and unavailing: they allow themselves to be mutilated, becoming armless, legless, featureless, in an effort to approximate to their quintessential "selves"; they stagger to a standstill, now bedridden, now propped up against walls, now stuck in vases like sheaves of flowers, in order to escape from the tyranny of movement and its despotic corollaries; or else they try to die, and dying, strive to detach their "selves" from the unhappy accident of incarnation, hoping thereby to redeem at last the catastrophe of spatial and temporal identity—only to discover that their "personality," against all the odds, survives.

The "I" in fact seems indestructible; it runs on from paragraph to paragraph, from novel to novel, from play to play, in endlessly-evolving monologues. And yet its current identity is never more than a mask, a pretext, a "pseudo-self," compounded of arbitrary experience and continuity in time and of words unwillingly learnt from others. If it is ever to know its "true" self, the "pseudo-self" must disappear, and all the borrowed words of which it is made up must vanish with it—yet, once words have vanished, how shall the timeless being that remains now know itself? How shall it say at long last "I am *I*," when all that constitutes the "I"—including the very word—has been discarded? It is the logical impossibility of the Sartrian *For-Itself* seeking to identify itself with the *In-Itself*, and yet retain its own awareness. It is the proverbial Guardsman, trying to lift himself up to the ceiling by pulling at his own boot-straps. Yet this, in Beckett's universe, is the condition of man. There he stands—or lies, or rolls—mutilated, miserable and helpless, waiting for an end which cannot come, searching for the resolution of his own enigma which, like the enigma of π, or of $\sqrt{-1}$,

---

[2] *Waiting for Godot*. London (Faber), 1956, p. 9.

must logically be capable of solution, yet which can never be resolved. "God have pity on me!" cries Estragon. At which Vladimir, vexed, enquires, "And me?" But Estragon feels too clearly his own tragic dilemma to care deeply about others: "On me! On me! Pity! On me!" [3]

If the human condition is thus intolerable, what sort of a God is responsible for it? What unspeakable Being has conjured up a creature who cannot know himself, yet cannot bear not to know himself, imprisoned for no knowable reason in a duration which cannot be endured? This is one of the problems—perhaps the central problem—of Beckett's whole work, from *Proust* and the early stories of *More Pricks Than Kicks*, to *How It Is* and *Happy Days*. His people, like Dostoievsky's, are "God-obsessed." They look at man, and conclude that God is unforgivable. If He exists, he is unforgivable for having made the world as it is, when any rational creature could have made it better. A tinker or a tailor could have made it better. "But my dear Sir," says the tailor in Nagg's story, "my dear Sir, look—(*disdainful gesture, disgustedly*)—at the world—(*pause*)—and look—(*loving gesture, proudly*)—at my TROUSERS!" [4] If He does not exist, whose fault is it? Not man's, certainly; therefore God's. Another incompetence. Once again, God is unforgivable. Moreover, both hypotheses are equally inconceivable. That God should have created a being rational enough to appreciate the flaws in his own constitution, and yet should have failed to remedy these flaws—for instance, by substituting a bicycle for the human frame—is hopelessly irrational, for then God would be simultaneously both good and evil, intelligent and unintelligent, all-powerful and not all-powerful . . . a logical impossibility, in which the opposites would cancel each other out, and the evidence for his existence would prove that he could not exist.[5] On the other hand, the materialist hypothesis is equally unacceptable. Beckett's people *know*, from the evidence of their own logic and their own experience, that temporal and spatial reality is an illusion, and that their "real" selves exist in another, non-material dimension. They live, like Belacqua, "in the interstices of reality," and they cannot conceive of an essentially non-material reality having its origins in the material laws of cause and effect, which laws it escapes at every point. In fact, if

[3] *Ibid.*, p. 77.
[4] *Endgame*. London (Faber), 1958, p. 22.
[5] The so-called "Manichæan solution," which posits the existence of two Gods, one of good and the other of evil, in eternal opposition, is one which never occurs to Beckett's people, for the simple reason that Beckett's final solution to the problem renders it unnecessary.

man is, in the broad sense, an absurdity, God is, in the logical sense, an impossibility, and it is just as impossible that He should not exist as that He should. And in either case, the fault is His. Hamm puts the case more strikingly. "Let us pray to God," he orders. There is a silence, at the end of which he concludes, "The bastard! He doesn't exist!"—an affirmation which is immediately qualified by Clov's "Not yet." [6] But even Hamm, who comes closer to despair than any other Beckettian character, is anything rather than an atheist in the accepted meaning of the word. Hamm's black fury is directed *at* God; God's non-existence is simply the last and dirtiest trick which the sadistic Creator has played on his victimised and miserable creation.

For Beckett's people, then, it is rarely a matter of making categorical affirmations about the existence or the non-existence of God. Typically, when Bom asks Pim whether he "believes in God," he receives the answer "Yes"; but when he presses his interrogation further: "Every day?" Pim retorts "No." [7] The average Beckettian character is preoccupied first and foremost with his own implacable anger; and the existence of the anger implies (provisionally) the existence of a Cause to be angry at. Inevitably, moreover, the closer the conception of "God," at any given moment, corresponds to the orthodox picture of "a personal God quaquaquaqua with white beard," [8] the more violent, bitter and merciless are the accusations directed at him. A God who could create a world of suffering, absurdity and death, and yet still give man an inherent notion of beauty, happiness and significance (164) can only be a Being so cruel and so utterly cynical as to pass all human understanding. Again and again, Beckett's characters reveal the "divine spark" in them by their causeless and wanton sadism. Vladimir and Estragon kick at the prostrate Lucky; Molloy knocks down the inoffensive charcoal-burner and then deals him "a good dint on the skull" (84); Lemuel, the Keeper in Macmann's "House of St John of God" (the name is not without significance), gives the impression of being "slightly more stupid than malevolent, and yet his malevolence was considerable" (266); while Sam and Watt, amusing themselves together one sunny, windy afternoon, put the Beckettian indictment in its clearest form:

[6] *Endgame*, pp. 37–38.
[7] *How It Is*. New York (Grove), 1964, p. 97.
[8] *Waiting for Godot*, p. 42.

Birds of every kind abounded, and these it was our delight to pursue, with stones and clods of earth. Robins in particular, thanks to their confidingness, we destroyed in great numbers. . . . But our particular friends were the rats . . . they would come flocking round us at our approach, with every sign of confidence and affection, and glide up our trouserlegs, and hang upon our breasts. And then we would sit down in the midst of them, and give them to eat, out of our hands, of a nice fat frog, or a baby thrush. Or seizing suddenly a plump young rat, resting in our bosom after its repast, we would feed it to its mother, or its father, or its brother, or its sister, or to some less fortunate relative.

It was on these occasions, we agreed after an exchange of views, that we came nearest to God.[9]

If such is the nature of God, Beckett seems to suggest, then most of the deliberate evil and stupidity in the world arises when man seeks to imitate him. To "be like God" is to be vain, jealous, malevolent, sadistic and half-witted. "Seeking to be God," concludes the Alba, glancing at Belacqua in the story *A Wet Night*, "in the slavish arrogance of a piffling evil";[10] nor has Beckett any doubt at any point of man's moral superiority to his Creator. It was man, not God, who discovered pity—a theme which is first encountered in *Dante and the Lobster*, and which recurs again and again in the later works.[11] God, on the other hand, has the advantage of man in having invented death. More than any other writer of his generation except perhaps Ionesco, Beckett is haunted by the problem of death, and in the majority of his writings, but particularly in the *Trilogy*, he is concerned to find, by rational analysis and without resorting to any form of revelation, Christian or otherwise, a meaning for that which obliterates all meaning, including its own, and an explanation for the inexplicable.

There are, however, two works which stand out from the rest, precisely in that they seek no explanation, but are content merely to consider the *fact* in the merciless light of objective scrutiny, and, having weighed the evidence well, to pronounce one of the most implacable arraignments against God—the god of death—that has ever been written. These are the story *Dante and the Lobster*, and the much later play for radio, *All That Fall*. *Dante and the Lobster* is simply a succes-

[9] *Watt*. Paris (Olympia Press), 1958, pp. 169–70.
[10] A Wet Night," in *More Pricks Than Kicks*. London (Chatto & Windus), 1934, p. 106.
[11] See especially: *More Pricks Than Kicks*, p. 15 ("Dante and the Lobster"); pp. 161–2 ("What a Misfortune!"); *En Attendant Godot*, Paris (Minuit), 1952, p. 140; *Endgame*, pp. 29, 49, etc.; *Comment C'est*, pp. 102, etc.

sion of images of death, with the stress laid heavily on the pain, the
futility and the cruelty of it: the face of "McCabe the assassin" glares
reproachfully from the page of the newspaper on which Belacqua cuts
his toast, the "Malahide murderer's" petition for mercy is rejected,
the lobster dies in boiling water, the Aunt is seen tending "whatever
flowers die at that time of the year," and even the moon bears on it
the face of Cain,

> that countenance, fallen and branded, seared with the first stigma of
> God's pity, that an outcast might not die slowly.[12]

The irony of Beckett's story is ferocious, the more so for being half-
concealed. Its underlying theme—the "pity" of a God of death, the
"pity," in Belacqua's phrase, "of a jealous God on Nineveh"—is echoed
by Signorina Ottolenghi (herself not the most sympathetic of God's
creatures) in the essay-subject which she sets Belacqua for his study of
Dante: "You might do worse than make up Dante's rare moments of
compassion in Hell." [13] Dante's blind, or almost blind concurrence
with the judgments of an appalling God appears to be one of the
aspects of the Italian poet which has never ceased to fascinate Beckett,
albeit Belacqua himself is borrowed, unexpectedly, not from the *Inferno* but from the *Purgatorio*. Yet even Dante—God's Commissar or
Quisling among men—has greater compassion than his master. In *All
That Fall*, where the scope of death is even wider, from the dead child
on the railway-line to the "dead" engine of Mr Slocum's car, from
the dead hen on the road ("Just one great squawk and then . . .
peace") to the dead leaves in the ditch and to Death itself come to
fetch the Maiden in Schubert's music which haunts the play, the
irony is rather more obvious, but none the less bitter for that. There
are echoes of Dante still—"Dante's damned, with their faces arsy-
versy" [14]—but here, God's representative is more specifically "the
Preacher," who adds to Dante's acceptance of the divine cruelty an
attribute more nauseating still: that of hypocrisy. This God who is the
God of evil, death and torture is at the same time forever ranting
about "mercy." "The Lord upholdeth all that fall, and raiseth up all
those that be bowed down." Old Dan and Maddy, having heard the
Preacher's text, "join in wild laughter." [15] If Dan *has* in fact murdered

[12] *More Pricks Than Kicks,* p. 5.
[13] *Ibid.,* p. 15.
[14] *All That Fall.* London (Faber), 1957, p. 29.
[15] *Ibid.,* p. 36.

the child who fell out of the train (the play itself leaves us in doubt at the end), there is in him for all that less evil than there is in God— for if he killed her, at least he did not invent death, nor did he first create in order to kill, nor did he prolong the suffering for his own pleasure, nor, finally, did he kill without a reason, as God does. The child was doomed anyway, and in Dan's twisted and cantankerous old mind, his act could be interpreted as that of saving an innocent "maiden" from the ignominious "doom" of life. Whereas Gaber's "employer," by contrast, is as imbecile as he is evil. "He does not know what he says," states Gaber. And then adds, "Nor what he does" (94f.).

We never meet the incumbent of the parish of Foxrock in *All That Fall*, nor, in fact, any of God's official representatives save for the worldly Father Ambrose, who makes a brief, ambiguous appearance in *Molloy* (99–102). Only one of Beckett's characters, moreover, is in any precise sense of the term religious: that mean and petty domestic tyrant, Moran. The actual practices of religion seem, by and large, to lie beneath the writer's contempt. By contrast, the subtleties of theological disputation and of scholastic argument appear to fascinate him, and in particular the Doctrine of Transubstantiation. "Would I be granted the body of Christ after a pint of Wallenstein?" muses Moran; "would the Eucharist produce the same effect, taken on top of beer, however light?" (97). A knotty problem; and one which had already come to the notice of Mr Dum Spiro, "editor of *Crux*, the popular Catholic monthly," when he drew from his pocket a letter from a sorely-puzzled reader:

Lourdes
Basses-Pyrénées
France

Sir,
    A rat, or other small animal, eats of a consecrated wafer.
    1) Does he ingest the Real Body, or does he not?
    2) If he does not, what has become of it?
    3) If he does, what is to be done with him?

Yours faithfully,
Martin Ignatius MacKenzie
(Author of *The Chartered Accountant's Saturday Night*)[16]

If there is a great deal of irony, once again, in episodes such as these,

---

[16] *Watt*, p. 30.

there is also a certain element of hesitation. For Beckett's people, God may well be a monstrous and inconceivable evil; but precisely because of the extent of this evil, it cannot be lightly dismissed. Beckett takes God as seriously as nuclear warfare. And the arguments concerning the nature and attributes of God have this in common with Beckett's own thought: they are extremely subtle and extremely learned, and they contain their own *reductio ad absurdum*. Repeatedly, we find Beckett's characters held spell-bound by the baroque convolutions of theological speculation. Murphy is a sometime theological student. The sight of the orthodox believer attempting to reduce the details of his belief to some sort of logical coherence evokes in Beckett, not only satirical humour, but also the echoes of a hidden sympathy; nor can it be denied that the doomed frustration of scholastic reason struggling to construct water-tight systems out of wholly unverifiable first-principles has much in common with Beckett's own "dialectic of incommensurables."

None the less, these by-roads of theological Aristotelianism, fascinating as they are, do not affect the main substance of Beckett's argument. The *methods* of knowing about God, whether comic or serious in themselves, cannot alter the fact that "God," as conceived by the orthodox, is the supreme manifestation of evil, and that this earth of ours, left to God's tender mercies, is doomed to face at the last an indescribable agony of destruction and death. In Beckett's earlier works, the central theme is the futile and purposeless death of the individual—of Murphy and Belacqua, or of the "old boy," the retired butler who commits suicide in Miss Carridge's lodgings. But in the later writings, although this theme is still present (especially in *Endgame*), the place of importance is gradually usurped by a broader understanding of God's cruelty—an apocalyptic vision, recurrent and terrifying, of the death, not of one man, but of Man, the senseless extinction, not of an individual life, but of all life, leaving a frozen or a burning planet to wander for all eternity in the absurd infinity of space. This, of course, is the main theme of Lucky's great monologue in *Waiting for Godot*, with its vision of "the earth in the great cold the great dark the air and the earth abode of stones in the great cold alas alas . . .";[17] but Molloy likewise listens, "and the voice is of a world collapsing endlessly, a frozen world under a faint untroubled sky,

---

[17] *Waiting for Godot,* p. 44.

enough to see by, yes, and frozen too" (40), while Malone and Bom both at different times see themselves suddenly as "the last of the living" in a dead or dying land. In the plays, it is the same. Bolton and Holloway, in *Embers,* meet in a "white world, great trouble, sound of dying, dying glow," [18] while Winnie's landscape is an arid and burning saltmarsh, whence the last of the grass has long since withered. But this vision of final, senseless, universal extinction reaches its climax in *Endgame,* for here, not only do Hamm and Clov represent the last of living things in a burnt-out landscape of stones and dust, but Hamm's strange anecdote of the mad artist condenses into a few lines the whole of Beckett's vision of the end of life:

> I once knew a madman who thought the end of the world had come. He was a painter—and engraver. I had a great fondness for him. I used to go and see him, in the asylum. I'd take him by the hand and drag him to the window. Look! There! All that rising corn! And there! Look! The sails of the herring fleet! All that loveliness! *(Pause).* He'd snatch away his hand and go back into his corner. Appalled. All he had seen was ashes. *(Pause).* He alone had been spared. *(Pause).* Forgotten. . . .[19]

Beckett's God, then, if his attributes are to be deduced from the *prima facie* evidence of his creatures, their sufferings and their destiny, is a Being so monstrous, mad and cruel, that man might even come to pity Him, as lunatics were to be pitied, or murderers, were they not so dangerous. But the originality of Beckett's thought is that this vision of evil and destruction represents not so much the conclusion of his argument, as its starting-point. Beckett gives us the evidence, and his people cry out against God—yet ultimately, they refuse to accept the evidence that they themselves have provided, and their indictment turns into an appeal for a different *kind* of God altogether, and with that, a different kind of death, a different kind of reality, a different kind of meaning. For, where all is absurd, meaningless and impossible, the only ultimate significance must be one which includes, or accepts, the meaninglessness of all recognized values and concepts. If "reality" —the everyday reality of fact, or matter, or personality, or belief— leads only to a state where "you pick yourself up and go on . . . cursing God and man," [20] then such a reality *cannot* be other than an

[18] *Embers.* London (Faber), 1959, p. 23.
[19] *Endgame,* p. 32.
[20] *From an Abandoned Work.* London (Faber), 1958, p. 19.

illusion. Behind "reality" lies the Void, the Nothing, "than which naught is more real"; and it is from this concept of the Void that Beckett's people start out on their pilgrimage in search of a new and more acceptable version of God.

In their unending quest for a new concept of the Self, and thus, ultimately, for a new concept of God, Beckett's people are at once hampered and encouraged by ideas and arguments inherited from the past. They are all, in a sense, mystics—that is, they are all aware of a force at work within them and about them, a force which goads them onwards towards ends which they themselves would not have envisaged, yet which can neither be analysed nor rationally explained, and which completely eludes the net of words. Moreover, they are all acutely conscious, as Watt is conscious, of the fact that no definition of God is possible, save in terms of that which he is *not:*

> For the only way one can speak of nothing is to speak of it as though it were something, just as the only way one can speak of God is to speak of him as though he were a man, which to be sure he was, in a sense, for a time, and as the only way one can speak of man, even our anthropologists have realised that, is to speak of him as though he were a termite.[21]

Their very failure, however, to find words adequate to embrace "reality," as they sense it to be, leaves them at the mercy of the symbolic vocabulary of other mystic cults—a vocabulary and a set of symbols that they find it all the more difficult to reject, in that it is always *possible* that the Christian or the Buddhist mystics were in fact trying to set down in their own terms experiences identical with those, say, of Hamm or Estragon or The Unnamable, and consequently, that this traditional symbolism may in fact be relevant to their own case. It is this which would seem to account for the fact that their conversation is sprinkled with references to traditional religious ideas, sometimes, admittedly, in a grotesque context (Sucky Molly, for instance, wears the Two Thieves as earrings, and carries Christ in her mouth: "A long yellow canine bared to the roots and carved, with the drill probably, to represent the celebrated sacrifice . . ." [264]), but only rarely in such terms as to indicate deliberate parody or disbelief. They have no interest in the practical or in the ethical aspects of Christianity—Macmann, like Molloy before him,

²¹ *Watt*, p. 84.

is satisfied with having "eluded charity all his days," and is "stunned" when it is forced upon him (256)—and if they have a very vivid and immediate interest in the state which awaits them after death, this "sotte éternité," in the words of the narrator of *Le Calmant*,[22] has little or nothing in common with the expectations of the average Christian believer. On the other hand, they all possess a strong feeling of being caught up in a pattern of salvation and damnation (" 'God blast you,' said Murphy. 'He is doing so,' replied Celia." [23]), of sin and redemption, above all of guilt and punishment, although it is at no point clear to them whether the punishment of life is brought about as the necessary consequence of some sin committed previously (such as that of "being born," as Vladimir suggests: the "original sin" of St Augustine or of Jansenius), or whether the laws of cause and effect in this case may not work backwards, in which case the *fact* of the punishment in the present may itself determine the existence of the sin in the past. Or alternatively, of course, the whole relationship may be completely arbitrary. "All here is sin," says The Unnamable, "you don't know why, you don't know whose, you don't know against whom, someone says to you . . ." (403f.); and Macmann experiences the same conviction:

And without knowing exactly what his sin was he felt full well that living was not a sufficient atonement for it or that this atonement was in itself a sin, calling for more atonement, and so on, as if there could be anything but life, for the living. And no doubt he would have wondered whether it was really necessary to be guilty in order to be punished but for the memory, more and more galling, of his having consented to live in his mother, then to leave her. And this again he could not see as his true sin, but as yet another atonement which had miscarried and, far from cleansing him of his sin, plunged him in it deeper than before. And truth to tell the ideas of guilt and punishment were confused together in his mind, as those of cause and effect so often are in the minds of those who continue to think. . . . (239f.)

Against this background of metaphysical uncertainty, the recurrent intrusion of Biblical imagery has a double significance. On the one hand, it represents a desperate attempt to define an indefinable awareness by using images and symbols which have been sanctified by the tradition of generations, and further, by exploring the meaning of

---

[22] "Le Calmant," in *Nouvelles et Textes pour Rien*. Paris (Minuit), 1955, pp. 44–45.
[23] *Murphy*, p. 7.

these symbols, to strive towards the reality behind them; on the other hand, they occur in moments of weakness, when the character, defeated by the anguish of the unavailing struggle with the absurd and the unknowable, momentarily gives up and flies for refuge to the comfort of orthodox belief, overwhelmed, like the narrator of *Texte pour Rien VI*, by the heart-breaking nostalgia for a faith he no longer possesses.[24] Sometimes—and notably in *Waiting for Godot*—both these attitudes are encountered simultaneously, although Vladimir, who is slightly more rationalistic than Estragon, tends to lay stress on the *interpretation* of his symbols (the Two Thieves, etc.), whereas Estragon, who is several degrees nearer to timelessness than his companion, is the more terrified of the two, and therefore more inclined to cling for safety to the traditional beliefs of a Christian heritage. Vladimir argues a moral from his text ("One of the two was saved. It's a reasonable percentage" [25]); Estragon, having finally lost his boots, prefers simply to identify himself with Christ who once walked barefoot.

The traditional symbolism, then, serves either as a refuge or as a short cut; and in both cases, its value is more than doubtful. As a refuge, it remains on the level of a sentimental "nostalgia" for a vanished faith, a sort of sublimated wishful-thinking; and considered as a short cut to a knowledge of ultimate reality, its value is at best ambiguous—the more so as Beckett himself seems uncertain how much weight to give it, and changes its significance, even in different versions of his own text. In the original (French) version of *Endgame*, for instance, the figure of the "child" seen through the window suggests at the same time Moses, Christ and the Buddha, whereas the later English version suggests merely the renewal of life on the dead planet; by contrast, Murphy, who, in his English version, lived in "a Mew in West Brompton," transposes his dwelling in French into "l'Impasse de l'Enfant-Jésus." Ultimately, however, Beckett's people come one and all to realize that they can never hope to "understand" God, His purpose, still less His lack of purpose ("God," says Malone, "does not seem to need reasons for what he does, and for omitting to do what he omits to do, to the same degree as his creatures, does he?" [245]), until they have understood something of themselves. And this

[24] *Nouvelles et Textes pour Rien,* p. 170.
[25] *Waiting for Godot,* p. 11.

alone absorbs most of the energies of their life, and of their death as well.

Alone among all Beckett's major characters, Murphy experiences the Void of self as something actively to be desired; for he alone adds to his background of Christian theology and second-generation Cartesianism at least a degree of proficiency in the techniques of Yoga—learned, presumably, from his one-time master, Neary, who himself had studied "somewhere north of the Nerbudda." [26] Not that Nirvana, within the framework of the Buddhist teachings, represents a state to be desired, for it is precisely that state which lies beyond desire; it is the *absence* of wish or will, the undifferentiated totality of Mind-Only from which all distinctions have been banished, the Nothing which can be neither invoked nor described nor conceived, yet from which all positive existence is ultimately derived: it is a dynamic negative, or, in the language of the Sutras, the "Plenum-Void." Yet Murphy, imperfect practitioner that he is, *does* contrive to desire that "nothing, that colourlessness which is such a rare post-natal treat," [27] and, at certain climactic moments in the novel, actually achieves it. For Murphy, the uncertain compromise between the logic of mathematics and the illogic of metaphysics, by some miracle, happens to work. He is aware, as no other Beckettian character is aware, of the actual "structure" of his mind—or of "what he liked to call his mind"—which structure he is able to translate into valid symbols; and these symbols serve as a link between a native rationalism equipped to grapple exclusively with positives, and the fundamental Void or negative which constitutes his inner Self.

Murphy's supreme virtue is his silence. Relying as he does largely on his visual symbols and his senses, he jettisons bit by bit the whole apparatus of intellect and thus manages to escape entanglement in the net of words. At first sight it seems that they elude him; in fact, however, it is he who eludes them. Watt, by contrast, is a thoroughgoing Wittgensteinian. Everything that *is,* so Watt believes, everything that has a finite, comprehensible reality, can be expressed in words; words alone, out of the "massive" and undifferentiated totality of the universe, can create "objects" or "meanings," "individualities" and "relationships." "Whereof one cannot speak, thereof one *must*

[26] *Murphy*, p. 3.
[27] *Ibid.*, p. 246.

be silent." [28] And Watt, whose faith in language is balanced by his
deep-seated fear of silence, reduces all problems that he comes across
to a formula of words—"and is comforted." Once he has found a
(verbal) explanation for any phenomenon, he is satisfied; he makes
himself "a pillow of old words, for a head." [29] Whether that explanation corresponds to any "reality," or whether there *is* any reality
other than that of the verbal universe, is a problem which is of no
interest to Watt. Watt lives exclusively by "face values," nor has he
"seen a symbol, nor executed an interpretation, since the age of four-
teen, or fifteen . . . whatever it was Watt saw, with the first look, that
was enough for Watt, that had always been enough for Watt, more
than enough for Watt." [30] But it is not enough for Beckett. Gradually,
Watt finds himself face to face with a series of incidents, for which
no verbal-logical explanation is possible (the "incident of the Galls,"
for instance), and finally with an absolute negative, or rather with a
"positive Void," symbolized by the enigmatic figure of Mr Knott. Watt's
overwhelming need is to give phenomena a reality by *naming* them;
yet his own name is an interrogation, while the name "Mr Knott,"
negative in any case by implication, has none but the most arbitrary
relationship to the reality behind it. It indicates what this reality "is
not," but it fails completely to define, still less to determine, what it
is. Thus, in the novel, Watt's positivism gradually cracks beneath the
dynamic and destructive power of negation, and his "reality of words"
disintegrates into a scattering of senseless, or quasi-senseless fragments:

Lit yad mac, ot og. Ton taw, ton tonk. Ton dob, ton trips. Ton vila,
ton deda. Ton kawa, ton pelsa. Ton das, ton yag. Os devil, rof mit.[31]

Watt's task is limited to registering the existence of this dynamic
negative; to account for it is beyond his powers, as it is likewise beyond his powers to locate it, save as being somewhere vaguely *outside*
himself, whether in "Mr Knott's house" or in "Mr Knott" himself. His
successors, however—the hero of the *Nouvelles,* Molloy, Moran, Malone, Macmann, Mahood, The Unnamable and the "I" of *Texts for
Nothing*—are engaged in burrowing ever more deeply into the inner

[28] Wittgenstein, L. *Tractatus Logico-Philosophicus.* London (Routledge & Kegan
Paul), 8th ed., 1960, p. 189.
[29] *Watt,* p. 128.
[30] *Ibid.,* p. 80.
[31] *Ibid.,* p. 183. Restored to a more "normal" order, this sentence reads: "So lived,
for time. Not sad, not gay. Not awake, not asleep. Not alive, not dead. Not body, not
spirit. Not Watt, not Knott. Till day came, to go."

recesses of their personality, there to discover a Void whose intangible, inaccessible reality is for ever withheld from them by the barrier of language. Out of words, they create themselves a "personality"—out of the words they speak, but also out of the inner language which constitutes "memory." Nor are these words even their own; they are learnt from others, not invented; not one iota of the "self" as known to the "I" who speaks or thinks is anything but a fake, an illusion constructed out of borrowed vocables. The "I" *feels* that there is a "true" self somewhere behind it or within it, yet it can never *think* about that self, because, in order to think, it must first clothe the negative in the positive disguise of language, and so transform it into something radically different from itself. The "self," once again, like all other aspects of ultimate reality, can only be described in terms of what it is not, and even to name it is already to distort it. That which is a Void, a negative, moreover, cannot be destroyed. It can, by a trick of linguistics, be transformed into a positive—but this positive is precisely what we call "life." The ultimate self, therefore, being a negative (The Unnamable's pseudo-identity, Worm, is a detailed imaginative interpretation of the Sartrian *Pour-Soi* in action), is simply not-life, and what is "not-life" logically cannot die. Molloy, like Hamm, hopes to die, but cannot. Malone, by a complex process of multiplying his various verbal personalities, contrives to detach his "I" from the pseudo-self he knows as Macmann, and then watches Macmann die—but this extraordinary feat of alienation still leaves the problem basically unresolved, for the death of "Macmann" is as powerless as the death of "Malone" to obliterate the apparently immortal "Pour-Soi" or negative principle. On the other hand, the ultimate self desperately needs an ending: partly in order to achieve its own final definition, partly in order to escape from the dimensions of time, space and language in order to know itself, partly again in order to "verify" its own existence, since, in Beckett's cosmogony, that which exists is determined just as rigorously by the cause of its ending acting retrospectively as it is by the cause of its beginning. And since death obviously cannot be the end, in this sense, what end can there be, save an ending of time itself, and an obliteration of space in the same instant?

Malone Dies is an imaginary experiment made with death and personality, whose object is to discover the relationship between "dying" and "ending." Malone's experiment fails, leaving The Unnamable— a Void-self, whose transient personality or personalities have "died" some time before—to struggle on vainly in search of that ending of time which alone can give him his final self-knowledge and self-definition. Like Vladimir and Estragon, like Hamm and Winnie, the new dimension towards which he is moving is that of an instantaneous present expanded into eternity; but as the moving instants slow down towards timelessness, their progressive deceleration means that they take longer and longer to reach their goal—and the nearer they get to that goal, the slower they approach it, so that, in a universe controlled by rational logic, it is strictly impossible that they should ever achieve it, despite the fact that reason may know that that goal in fact exists. Two symbols dominate both the *Trilogy* and the plays: Zeno's parable of the "little heap of millet," progressively augmented by *half* the quantity remaining to be added from the total (this becomes the "little heap of days" in *Endgame* and Winnie's mound in *Happy Days*); and secondly, the recurring decimal or irrational number (Moran's son's dentist bears the characteristic name of Mr Pi), which proceeds by ever-decreasing degrees towards a logically definable objective, which objective, however, it can only reach when zero becomes a positive number. A "positive zero" would be, in fact must be, the solution to the Beckettian riddle. We know that, of necessity, it must exist; we know equally well that we can never reach it ("you must go on, I can't go on, you must go on, I'll go on," says The Unnamable, "you must go on, I can't go on, I'll go on" [414]); and meanwhile, we can but wait, caught up in an anguish of impossibilities— wait for the end of the decimal, or the completion of the heap, for the materialization of the dynamic Void, or whatever we like to call it. For of course, whatever we call it, it remains by definition that which cannot be defined, except in terms irrelevant to itself. So why not call it (provisionally) "Mr Knott" . . . or "Godot"?

Beckett's people, then, are one and all beings striving to realize, or at least to have knowledge of, the Void of their inner selves, and at the same time, driven by some wholly irrational force, they are seeking to establish some sort of correlation between this microcosmic self and the macrocosm outside themselves—the Buddha's "Plenum-Void"—just as Murphy seeks to realize, in the padded cells of the Magdalen Mental Mercyseat, an equivalent of that "closed circuit" which is his own inner existence. And once The Unnamable has established beyond any manner of doubt the truth that the Void of self is that which eludes all rational definition, and therefore cannot be named, it inevitably begins to dawn on his successors, the narrators of *Texts for*

Nothing and *How It Is,* that "God" likewise is an absolute-unnamable, whose reality is radically distorted as soon as a name or a concept is attached to him. And of all the "attributes" gratuitously accorded to this ultimate of Not-Being by our pseudo-selves in the domain of being, the most dangerous by far is that of "existence."

Which brings us back to the problem "does God exist?" This is a question to which, quite logically, Beckett's people cannot reply—or rather, being human, they reply in contradictions. Either they answer "no," and proceed to act as though he did, or else they reply "yes," and act as though he did not. In fact, of course, the question is meaningless. For to assert in so many words "God does not exist" is to assert nothing either way about the existence of God. If "that which exists" is that which is positive, or finite, or definable, or in any way verbally to be differentiated from other existent or non-existent phenomena, then "God," void, infinite, undifferentiated and abstracted from the dimensions of time and space, is precisely "that which does not exist." Nirvana is "that which does not exist"; it is the liberation of the finite by the infinite. Alfred Jarry, in writing the concluding lines of *Dr Faustroll,* seems to have been arguing to himself along the same lines when he concluded: "God is the tangential point of Zero and the Infinite" . . . which at least is an admirable definition of Godot. By contrast, to *name* God (as does the Preacher in *All That Fall*), to define his attributes, to circumscribe his essential Not-Being as though it were a positive phenomenon which could be imprisoned in words and in the logic of time and space, is to distort the Absolute into a false-absolute, or pseudo-God, just as logic and language, by an identical process, create out of the ultimate self a "pseudo-self" called "I" or "Macmann" or "Mahood" or "Worm." And for Beckett's people, that which is a lie (and *all* words are lies) is unendurable. The essential self is timeless and deathless; but the "I," the "self" I know, is condemned to death, to unbelievable suffering, mutilation and absurdity, and this gratuitous futility and misery can only have been ordained by the cruel caprices of a "God" who is himself of the same element—words—and who understands what he is inflicting. The "true God" can only be a macrocosmic equivalent of the microcosmic Void of the "true self"; the Preacher's "God"—a God who is conceivable—can be nothing but a malevolent and monstrous projection of the pseudo-self, or, in Sartrian terms, either of the "In-Itself" or of the "Other." If there is a total reality (as all Beckett's people realize there must be), it is the

eternal *Pour-Soi,* the Absolute Unnamable; as soon as the Preacher
calls on "God," and says what he will or will not do, all he does is
to create a corresponding *En-Soi* (the Void's own pseudo-self or "vice-
exister"), concocted out of human words and reflecting human evil.
Even Moran already knew as much:

> And I would never do my bees the wrong I had done my God, to whom
> I had been taught to ascribe my angers, fears, desires, and even my
> body. (169)

It is the Preacher's God who is the God of death, destruction and
torture. He upholdeth no-one. Only the wordless self, and not the
Preacher, may perhaps go beyond death, to the very brink of another
reality.

This deduction by inference of a God who is not in a mystic but in
a logical sense "unnamable," of an "incommensurable" which, like
$\sqrt{2}$, must necessarily exist and yet equally necessarily can never be
known, would seem to offer a neat and final solution to the Beckettian
problem, beyond which there is no need to go. And if Moran, say, or
Mahood, is constantly aware of the compulsive force of the Absolute,
this is simply because—in a complete non-Christian sense—"God" is
already within him. For just as, in the search for a dimension beyond
time, the absolute-instantaneous and the eternal-timeless coincide and
merely constitute alternative aspects of an identical awareness, so the
Void of the self coincides with, or indeed *is,* the Void of the Absolute.
When the whole is zero, the part may be just as great, if not greater
than the whole. Beckett's people, however, do not stop at this point.
With their indefatigable appetite for metaphysical impossibilities, they
lurch forward into an abyss of argument and speculation so baroque
that it is hard to know whether to take it seriously. Yet Beckett is a
serious writer, and none of his mystifications are to be taken lightly.

Beginning with *Molloy,* two forces combine to harass and bewilder
Beckett's people; on the one hand, that obscure sense of compulsion
within themselves, that "hypothetical imperative" which compels Molloy, for instance, to write down so many pages of his experiences every
week, or sends Moran out on his fruitless travels, or forbids poor
Winnie to lower her parasol, or even to arrange her hat:

> To think there are times one cannot take off one's hat, not if one's life
> was at stake. Times one cannot put it on, times one cannot take it
> off. . . .[32]

[32] *Happy Days* London (Faber), 1961, p. 20.

—on the other hand, there is the malevolent power of language which builds an impenetrable barrier between reality as it can be known, and the ultimate reality as it is. In the case of Belacqua, or Watt, or Murphy, the "imperative" was obscurely felt, rather than heard; but with Molloy and Moran, it begins to take the form of an inner "voice":

> I am still obeying orders, if you like, but no longer out of fear. No, I am still afraid, but simply from force of habit. And the voice I listen to needs no Gaber to make it heard. For it is within me, and exhorts me to continue to the end the faithful servant I have always been, of a cause that is not mine. . . . (131f.)

Molloy, all in all, accepts his "voice" as a force in his existence without enquiring too deeply into its origins; but Moran begins to hate it, "with hatred in my heart, and scorn, of my master and his designs" (132), and this hatred grows into an obsession in the case of The Unnamable. For since all thought is words, the only "self" that "I" can know is compounded out of words, and out of other peoples' words into the bargain, since all words are learnt from others. These "others," consequently, determine the person that I am, both to myself and to the rest of the world (in *Waiting for Godot,* it is these same "others" who beat up Estragon, night after night), and to The Unnamable, it seems that he is tyrannized by a malevolent committee known as "they," whose voices supply every word that he speaks, even those words which recognize and disown "them." "I say what I am told to say," he notes, "in the hope that some day they will weary of talking at me" (345); and later:

> They say they, speaking of them, to make me think that it is I who am speaking. Or I say they, speaking of God knows what, to make me think that it is not I who am speaking. (370)

This enforced alienation of the self into the hands of a hostile and elusive congregation of "others" who, by their very existence, render impossible any real existence for the self, is an ever-present source of despair and anguish for The Unnamable. However, the "I" of *How It Is,* faced with the same problem, begins to see the glimmering of a solution. The essential self, he argues, has, and can have, no "voice" of its own. It is the "I," the pseudo-self, that possesses a voice, but like The Unnamable it can only learn its words from others—in the event, from Pim, the strange "companion" whose alternate absences and presences form the subject of the novel—and thus, in a literal sense, it *becomes* the words that Pim is made to speak. It is Pim who gives it an existence in time and space, "up there in the light." But, since this existence, this "life," is conjured up by another's words, the "other" necessarily shares this life. It is a common life, a common voice, between the two of them. In the endless chain of being, however, which stretches from infinite past to infinite future, the "I" (Bom) will at some time or other be required to teach the words he has learnt to another, and this other to yet another, and so on. Each passes to his neighbour that basic vocabulary which, in due course, creates the experience of self and the evidence of life in time. The situation, therefore, is no longer that of The Unnamable, who was tyrannized into life in time by his "committee" of independent voices; the self of *How It Is* participates in a single, universal voice:

> quaqua the voice of us all who all those here before me and to come alone in this wallow. . . .[83]

—a voice eternal, unceasing, which at the same time *may* be (after all) merely his own voice all the time:

> my voice otherwise nothing therefore nothing otherwise my voice therefore my voice so many words strung together. . . .[84]

Thus once again the unique-instantaneous and the universal-infinite coincide: the single voice of the self, and the universal voice of conscious awareness. Yet (moderately logically) one may argue, as Bom argues, that a "universal voice" is inconceivable without a corresponding "universal ear." Speech (as an absolute) without a listener is unimaginable: a means of communication presupposes the existence of someone to communicate with, otherwise the very concept is absurd:

> an ear above somewhere above and unto it the murmur ascending . . .
> an ear a mind to understand a means of noting a care for us . . . immemorial imperishable like us the ear we're talking of an ear. . . .[85]

Thus, step by step, Beckett is led to postulate the existence of a "God"—a "God" whose existence is as it were determined by the existence of language. We find a variant of the same argument in *Happy Days*, where Winnie "proves" that Willie must necessarily be present,

---

[83] *How It Is*, pp. 107f.
[84] *Ibid.*, p. 95.
[85] *Ibid.*, pp. 134f.

even when she cannot see him, even when she may presume him (from other evidence) to be dead and gone, since she is talking to him, the fact of speech once more implying, in a still-logical universe, the ultimate necessity of a listener:

> I used to think. . . . I say I used to think that I would learn to talk alone. . . . By that I mean to myself, in the wilderness. . . . But no. . . . No no. . . . Ergo you are there. . . . Oh no doubt you are dead, like the others, no doubt you have died, or gone away and left me, like the others, it doesn't matter, you are there. . . .[36]

The implications of this argument would seem to be that the existence of language not merely determines the attributes and the "life" of man, but also determines at least one positive attribute in God: "God" is he who can listen. Or else, that words can only have their origin in The Word. This hypothesis is fascinating, although it must not be forgotten that, in *How It Is,* every positive statement or hypothesis is at some point cancelled out by its corresponding negative. In spite of Bom's subsequent denials of all that he has previously asserted, however, we are left with the strong impression that Beckett's argument, in some way or other, still holds good. It is the Biblical "In the Beginning was the Word," interpreted in terms of Wittgensteinian logical positivism and Sartrian epistemology, which now leads to the conclusion that, just as the Self is the inconceivable *Néant* of silence behind the words of language, so also "God" is the Total Nothing behind The Word which is creation—and that, between the *Pour-Soi* and Nirvana, the link is simply common speech! This conclusion, moreover, seems to be reinforced by the recurrent insistence, in Beckett's later works, on the theme of "prayer." "Our Father which art . . ."[37] begins Nagg. "For Jesus Christ's sake, Amen," begins Winnie in Act I of *Happy Days,* although by Act II, something seems to have gone wrong: "I used to pray . . . I say I used to pray . . . yes, I must confess I did. . . . Not now. . . . No no. . . ."[38] The "I" of *How It Is* seems to be in similar difficulties; for, if the haunting figure of the "kneeling tramp" is one of the most striking symbolic images in the novel, Bom himself is more uncertain of the process: "maudire Dieu, le bénir, l'implorer, aucun son . . ."—uncertain whether the only alternative to words is The Word . . . or silence.

[36] *Happy Days,* pp. 37–38.
[37] *Endgame,* p. 38.
[38] *Happy Days,* p. 38.

Twenty years earlier, however, Murphy had already been struggling with the same problem: "In the Beginning was the Word." But for Murphy, as indeed for all Beckett's people, the only supremely satisfying form of language is the *pun*—the absurdity of words turned in upon themselves, where meanings cancel each other out and leave yet another *Néant,* a sudden reverberating silence within the "big blooming buzzing confusion" of sound and significance, a little padded cell of anti-language, where Murphy feels deliciously at home. "In the beginning was the Pun." [39] When plus and minus cancel each other out, the result is Nothing. The Word is Nothing. The Self is Nothing. And only Nothing is real.

Obviously Beckett is no more an "atheist" in the blunt materialistic sense than he is an orthodox Christian, as certain interpretations of *Godot* have tried to demonstrate. He belongs to that "Ecole du Néant" which is such a remarkable feature of contemporary French philosophy and literature, and of which Existentialism is no more than a particularly flamboyant branch. His philosophy is at bottom that of the mystic: *Credo quia impossibile est*; only he happens to be a rationalist for whom "the impossible" is not the alternative to a logic which has failed, but the inevitable conclusion of a logic which has succeeded.

A "God" who can be made the subject of any positive definition is, for Beckett, a God of words or falsehood, a pseudo-God—quite as "real," perhaps, as the "pseudo-selves" of our conceptual personalities, but essentially a God made in the image of the Preacher: a God of evil, cruelty and death. A God whose existence is as unforgivable as his non-existence. On the other hand, Beckett's awareness of man as an impossible anomaly in time and space, together with his sense of the "positive Void" which lies for ever out of reach behind the bland façades of "self" and "personality," leads him necessarily to postulate a similar "Plenum-Void" behind the Word which is the God we can conceive. With "words" as the link between the two. Or if not words, then possibly—just possibly—music. The stream of "music, *music,* MUSIC," which is the symbol of Murphy's love for Celia, runs underground for nearly twenty years, to reappear, muddied and diminished but unmistakable, in *All That Fall* and *Krapp's Last Tape* and *Happy Days.* Music can go where words cannot . . . even to the "wellhead":

---

[39] *Murphy,* p. 65.

Then down a little way
Through the trash
Towards where
All dark no begging
No giving no words
Through the scum
Down a little way
To whence one glimpse
Of that wellhead [40]

And the "wellhead" may be the "Self" or may be "God": the instantaneous-present or the eternal-timeless, which after all, for Beckett's people, are only alternative aspects of the identical mystery.

[40] *Words and Music.* In *Evergreen Review,* No. 27, Nov.–Dec., 1962, p. 42.

Chronology of Important Dates

	Beckett	*The Age*
1904–5		Russo-Japanese War.
1906	Born in Foxrock, near Dublin, Good Friday, April 13.	
1912		First Balkan War.
1913		Second Balkan War.
1914–18		World War I.
1917		Two Russian revolutions; tsar deposed, Bolsheviks seize control.
1919		League of Nations founded.
1922		*Ulysses* published. Death of Proust.
1927	B.A. in French and Italian, Trinity College, Dublin.	
1928–30	Lecteur d'Anglais, Ecole Normale Supérieure, Paris.	1928: Italy becomes fascist dictatorship under Mussolini.
1929	"Dante . . . Bruno. Vico. . Joyce," in *Our Exagmination round his Factification for Incamination of Work in Progress.*	Depression.
1930	*Whoroscope,* prize-winning poem on Descartes.	

1931   *Proust.*

1932–36   Lives   in   London,   travels   1932: General MacArthur scat-
                through Europe.   ters Bonus Army marching on
                                                           Washington. 1933: Hitler be-
                                                           comes German chancellor. 1936:
                                                           Spanish Civil War begins.

1934   *More Pricks Than Kicks* (ten
                short stories).

1935   *Echo's Bones and Other Precip-
                itates* (poems).

1937   Settles in Paris.

1938   *Murphy.*

1939   League of Nations founders.
                                                           Death of Yeats.

1939–45   World War II.

1941   Death of Joyce.

1942   In hiding in the Vaucluse, near
                Avignon. Begins *Watt.*

1945   United Nations founded. Peace
                                                           begins, i.e., racial and social
                                                           clashes, undeclared wars, etc.

1945   Returns to Paris. Writes *Nou-
                velles (L'Expulsé, Le Calmant,
                La Fin)* and *Mercier et Camier*
                (unpublished novel).

1946–49   Writes the trilogy in French.
                October 1948–1949, writes *En
                attendant Godot.*

1949   *Three Dialogues* (on painters
                and aesthetics).

1951   *Molloy* and *Malone meurt* pub-
                lished.

1952   *En attendant Godot* published.

1953   *Watt* and *L'Innomable* pub-
                lished.

1955	*Nouvelles et Textes pour rien* published.
1957	*Fin de partie (Endgame)* performed and published.
1961	*Comment c'est (How It Is)* published.
1964	*Film* produced.
1965	Death of T. S. Eliot.
1969	Wins Nobel Prize.

Notes on the Editor and Contributors

J. D. O'HARA, editor of this volume, teaches at the University of Connecticut.

RICHARD N. COE is Professor of French at the University of Melbourne and the author of *Samuel Beckett, Eugene Ionesco,* and *The Vision of Jean Genêt,* among others.

FRANCO FANIZZA is an Italian critic of modern literature.

JOHN FLETCHER is Professor of Comparative Literature, School of European Studies, University of East Anglia, and the author of two books on Beckett.

NORTHROP FRYE is one of the most influential of modern critics, and teaches at the University of Toronto. He is the editor of *Blake: A Collection of Critical Essays* (1966) in the Twentieth Century Views series.

LUDOVIC JANVIER teaches at the Université de Paris-Vincennes; he has published three critical works, one on the *nouveau roman, Une Parole Exigeante* (1964), and two on Beckett: *Pour Samuel Beckett* (1966) and *Beckett par lui-même* (1969). He is also the author of a novel, *La Baigneuse* (1968); with Beckett and A. Janvier, he translated *Watt* into French.

EDITH KERN is a critic of modern literature; she teaches at the University of Washington. She is the editor of *Sartre: A Collection of Critical Essays* (1962) in the Twentieth Century Views series.

Selected Bibliography

The serious student is urged to consult Raymond Federman and John Fletcher's *Samuel Beckett: His Works and His Critics* (Berkeley: University of California Press, 1970) for complete information.

Richard N. Coe, *Samuel Beckett* (New York: Grove Press, 1964), John Fletcher, *The Novels of Samuel Beckett* (London: Chatto & Windus, 1964), and Hugh Kenner, *Samuel Beckett: A Critical Study* (New York: Grove Press, 1961) provide valuable introductions to Beckett's work; the first two contain separate chapters on the trilogy. Michael Robinson, *The Long Sonata of the Dead* (London: Rupert Hart-Davis, 1969; New York: Grove Press, 1970) is a more recent survey that makes much use of earlier criticism. Ludovic Janvier's *Pour Samuel Beckett* (Paris: Editions de Minuit, 1966) contains more analysis of the trilogy than is reprinted here. G. C. Barnard, *Samuel Beckett: A New Approach* (New York: Dodd, Mead, & Co., 1970) considers Beckett's characters psychologically, primarily as schizophrenics. Ruby Cohn, *Samuel Beckett: The Comic Gamut* (New Brunswick, N. J.: Rutgers University Press, 1962) offers many useful insights. John Fletcher's *Samuel Beckett's Art* (London: Chatto & Windus, 1967) is not primarily about the trilogy but is often relevant. Olga Bernal, *Langage et fiction dans le roman de Beckett* (Paris: Gallimard, 1969) considers philosophical and linguistic problems in Beckett's work, with particular attention to *Watt* and *The Unnamable*.

Valuable essay collections include the Beckett issue of *Perspective*, ed. Ruby Cohn (1959); *Samuel Beckett Now*, ed. M. J. Friedman (Chicago: University of Chicago Press, 1970); *Samuel Beckett: A Collection of Critical Essays*, ed. Martin Esslin (Englewood Cliffs, N. J.: Prentice-Hall, Inc., 1965); and forthcoming collections by Raymond Federman (Paris: L'Herne) and David Hayman (Beckett issue of the *James Joyce Quarterly*, Winter, 1970–71).

Referred to in the editor's introduction were four interviews: Gabriel D'Aubarède, in *Nouvelles Litteraires* (Paris, 16 February 1961); Tom Driver, "Beckett by the Madeleine," *Columbia University Forum*, vol. 4 (Summer, 1961); Israel Shenker, "Moody Man of Letters," *New York Times*, Sec. 2 (Sunday, 6 May 1956); and Harold Hobson, "Samuel Beckett: Dramatist of the

Year," *International Theatre Annual,* vol. 1 (London, 1956). Also P. H. Solomon, "Samuel Beckett's *Molloy:* A Dog's Life," *French Review,* vol. 41 (1967) and Samuel Beckett, *En attendant Godot,* ed. Colin Duckworth (London: George G. Harrap & Co., 1966).

TWENTIETH CENTURY
INTERPRETATIONS

MAYNARD MACK, *Series Editor*
Yale University

NOW AVAILABLE
Collections of Critical Essays
ON

ADVENTURES OF HUCKLEBERRY FINN
ALL FOR LOVE
THE AMBASSADORS
ARROWSMITH
AS YOU LIKE IT
BLEAK HOUSE
THE BOOK OF JOB
THE CASTLE
CORIOLANUS
DOCTOR FAUSTUS
DON JUAN
DUBLINERS
THE DUTCHESS OF MALFI
ENDGAME
EURIPIDES' ALCESTIS
THE FALL OF THE HOUSE OF USHER
A FAREWELL TO ARMS
THE FROGS
GRAY'S ELEGY
THE GREAT GATSBY
GULLIVER'S TRAVELS
HAMLET
HARD TIMES
HENRY IV, PART ONE
HENRY IV, PART TWO
HENRY V
THE ICEMAN COMETH
INVISIBLE MAN
JULIUS CAESAR
KEATS'S ODES
LIGHT IN AUGUST
LORD JIM
MAJOR BARBARA

(continued on next page)

(continued from previous page)

MEASURE FOR MEASURE
THE MERCHANT OF VENICE
MOLL FLANDERS
MOLLOY, MALONE DIES, THE UNNAMABLE
MUCH ADO ABOUT NOTHING
THE NIGGER OF THE "NARCISSUS"
OEDIPUS REX
THE OLD MAN AND THE SEA
PAMELA
A PASSAGE TO INDIA
THE PLAYBOY OF THE WESTERN WORLD
THE PORTRAIT OF A LADY
A PORTRAIT OF THE ARTIST AS A YOUNG MAN
THE PRAISE OF FOLLY
PRIDE AND PREJUDICE
THE RAPE OF THE LOCK
THE RIME OF THE ANCIENT MARINER
ROBINSON CRUSOE
ROMEO AND JULIET
SAMSON AGONISTES
THE SCARLET LETTER
SIR GAWAIN AND THE GREEN KNIGHT
SONGS OF INNOCENCE AND OF EXPERIENCE
SONS AND LOVERS
THE SOUND AND THE FURY
THE TEMPEST
TESS OF THE D'URBERVILLES
TOM JONES
TO THE LIGHTHOUSE
TWELFTH NIGHT
THE TURN OF THE SCREW AND OTHER TALES
UTOPIA
VANITY FAIR
WALDEN
THE WASTE LAND
WOMEN IN LOVE
WUTHERING HEIGHTS